RAPTURE

NICK NURSE'S COACHING JOURNEY

1989: Assistant, University of Northern Iowa
1990: Player-Coach, Derby Rams (UK)
1991: Head Coach, Grand View University
1993: Assistant Coach, University of South Dakota
1995: Head Coach, Birmingham Bullets (UK)
1998: Head Coach, Telindus Oostende (Belgium)
1998: Head Coach, Manchester Giants (UK)
2000: Head Coach, London Towers (UK)
2001: Assistant Coach, Oklahoma Storm
2001: Head Coach, Brighton Bears (UK)
2005: Assistant Coach, Oklahoma Storm
2007: Head Coach, Iowa Energy
2009: Assistant Coach, Great Britain National Team
2011: Head Coach, Rio Grande Valley Vipers
2013: Assistant Coach, Toronto Raptors
2018: Head Coach, Toronto Raptors
2019: Head Coach, Canada National Team

RAPTURE

FIFTEEN TEAMS, FOUR COUNTRIES, ONE NBA CHAMPIONSHIP, AND HOW TO FIND A WAY TO WIN—DAMN NEAR ANYWHERE

NICK NURSE

WITH MICHAEL SOKOLOVE AND BRANDON HURLEY

FOREWORD BY PHIL JACKSON

Little, Brown and Company

New York Boston London

Little, Brown and Company
Hachette Book Group
1290 Avenue of the Americas, New York, NY 10104
littlebrown.com

First Edition: September 2020

Little, Brown and Company is a division of Hachette Book Group, Inc. The Little, Brown name and logo are trademarks of Hachette Book Group, Inc.

The publisher is not responsible for websites (or their content) that are not owned by the publisher.

The Hachette Speakers Bureau provides a wide range of authors for speaking events. To find out more, go to hachettespeakersbureau.com or call (866) 376-6591.

ISBN 978-0-316-54017-9
LCCN 2020933472

10 9 8 7 6 5 4 3 2 1

LSC-C

Printed in the United States of America

To Roberta, Noah, Leo, and Rocky
Your love lifts me higher . . .

In memory of
Maurice, Marcella, and Maureen
better known as
Maury, Mac, and Been
Not a day goes by when I don't miss each one of you . . .

CONTENTS

FOREWORD BY PHIL JACKSON

CORN-BRED AND CORN-FED

Nick Nurse came out of his rental pickup with a big grin on his face and extended his hand. "Never thought the beauty of Montana was this grand," he said. We shook, and I asked him to get into my truck for a drive around Flathead Lake. The trip is really quite long—it's a big lake. We made an early stop at a fruit stand and got a bag of washed cherries. Our conversation centered around people we knew but quickly got down to basketball. The sport is not the center of Nick Nurse's life, although he takes it very seriously.

I titled this foreword "Corn-Bred and Corn-Fed," but I don't mean that condescendingly. Nick exhibits his Midwestern sensibility quite naturally, even though he had to travel many roads to many places before he was given the chance to coach an NBA team. You even get the feeling that coaching *any* team is fine by him. Just look at his résumé and you'll see the wide variety of basketball venues he successfully competed in before he finally got a shot at coaching in the NBA.

I first heard of Nick a few years ago from Alex McKechnie. Part of the triumvirate of medical support staff with my old team, the Los Angeles Lakers, Alex had come to LA—joining Gary Vitti, a long established Laker trainer, and Chip Schaefer, who was with me for all eleven of my titles—to help Shaq recover from an abdominal tear in the late 1990s, and he was then recruited to join the Lakers full-time in 2001. When the Lakers staff disbanded in 2011 before the lockout season, the training staff was released, except for Vitti. Alex found employment in Toronto, which was no surprise. We stayed in contact, and when Nick Nurse joined the Raptors staff, Alex had a lot of good things to say about him. Alex brokered the visit by Nurse to Flathead Lake after Nick was named head coach of the Toronto team in the summer of 2018. So here we were driving around the lake, eating cherries, talking hoops, and enjoying the day.

Nick let me know he had studied the triangle offense back in the day. In fact, he had watched the first practice I had with the Lakers at their summer camp in Long Beach back in 1999. At the time, he was just a young coach, but he was absorbing as much b-ball as he could find. During our drive, we talked about the advent of the present game with nary a post-up player cluttering the lane. The stats "just verify" the fact that three-point shots have supplanted two-point shots. I argued that even if 33 percent of made threes is the score equal of 50 percent made twos, 66 percent of those threes are still misses, which makes rebounding and transition defense risky. Offensive rebounds become a "maybe" thing and full-court pressure defense becomes impossible. "What becomes the basis of a sound offense?" I asked. I give Nick credit for taking the bait. He explained that his tenure with the Rio Grande Vipers of the NBA D-League gave him the chance to make a system out of three-point shooting.

Passing and movement were still priorities. It wasn't all dribble and screen-and-roll.

We went back and forth for the rest of the ride around the lake and then at lunch at a roadside diner. Later that night we had dinner and talked more in terms of managing players, which is a very important skill in NBA coaching. How does a coach develop the confidence of the team? Nick's personality and ability to be a known entity to his players were real positives in his move to the head chair.

^

Nick asked me to write this foreword and I was happy to do so. His book will give you a good idea of the dedication and focus it takes to win as a coach. He does have that Midwest sensibility and hard work ethic, not to mention a variety of interests. For example, he taught himself how to play the piano and has a love of Thelonious Monk's genius. He even named his offense the Monk Offense (similar to Ron Ekker's) for its freestyle methods.

Coaching takes or makes a strong personality—one that understands that the coach is where the buck stops. This takes grit. Coaches have to point out the elephants in the room. Sometimes they take risks to bring players around to making changes in their game or in the team's. They have to have the verve to give the team confidence that everything is going to work out when things aren't going smoothly. When situations are tenuous and there is a victory or defeat in the balance, they must be calm enough to allow the players to relax and enjoy the moment. Nick's passion is evident, and his decisiveness during the pressure of last year's playoffs bodes well for his continued success. He just wants to coach.

Just before the 2020 All-Star Game, the Raptors were on a tear with a fifteen-game winning streak that has confounded basketball experts. After they lost Kawhi Leonard in free agency at the end of the previous season, experts thought the team would have trouble finishing in the top ranks, but Nick has made a career out of proving people wrong. Kudos to Nick Nurse—he can coach.

March 2020

RAPTURE

PROLOGUE

When I was twenty-two years old, just out of college and with a degree in accounting I was not excited about putting to use, I decided to give pro basketball a try. I was not anybody's idea of an NBA player. I could really shoot the ball—in four years at the University of Northern Iowa, I made 47 percent of my three-point attempts—but I was just six feet tall and, by the standards of high-level basketball, athletically deficient. Years later, my former college coach, Eldon Miller, paid me what I believe he meant as a compliment. "Nurse couldn't run very fast and couldn't jump at all," he told a reporter, before adding that I was an intelligent type who did not make many mistakes.

Through a friend in Iowa City who had connections in South America, I got an offer to play in Brazil, but their economy was collapsing, and the opportunity quickly vanished. I put together a résumé, cover letter, and some newspaper clippings about my playing career, figured out how much postage to put on the envelopes (this was 1990), and sent packets to pro clubs in Europe, Australia, and Japan.

The global basketball world was not nearly as connected then, and it wasn't obvious how to get on a roster. I thought I had a job with a team in Bonn, Germany, but then nothing came of it. Soon after, I received a letter from the owner of a team in Derby, England, a place I'd never heard of, saying they would like me to play point guard for them. That same day, the team's owner, a man named Tim Rudge, reached me by phone to tell me that in addition to playing, he wanted me to be the head coach.

Later, he would let me know he also expected me to score twenty points a game.

Two days later, I flew from Chicago with another American they had signed, Ernest Lee, who would provide one of my first lessons in international basketball: however far removed you may think you are from the main basketball grid, you'll be with some talent. Lee was a high school legend from Sacramento, a six-foot-four, broad-shouldered scoring machine who averaged thirty-four points a game at his Division II school, Clark Atlanta University.

The day after our arrival, we had a game. I was still learning the names of my players, and if we had a practice first, I don't remember it.

The home court of the Derby Rams was a community center that held no more than 1,500 people, and we had to roll the bleachers out before games. We only had access to the gym for practice twice a week, at seven P.M. A badminton club was in there before us, and as soon as they stopped hitting, we sort of stormed the court. The other days, I lifted weights, ran, and practiced shooting at a local health club after first paying a daily entry fee of eighty pence.

My job had other expectations. We were required to drink in a local pub with fans after home games. Normally, the coach would drive the team van to away games, but I was too young to legally operate a vehicle of that size, so I sat beside our center, a nice guy named Martin Ford, as he drove.

One night on one of our most distant road trips, to Newcastle, we broke down at like three in the morning and had to hike up a dark hill to a pay phone, and I remember asking myself, "Where the fuck am I?" and "What am I even doing here?"

That first job, player-coach in Derby, feels in some ways like a long time ago. I had a mop of sandy blond hair and still looked like I was seventeen years old. All I really knew how to do was lead by example, like the team captain I'd been all through my youth. In practices, I tried to win every wind sprint and shooting drill. In games, I played extremely hard.

But the experience is ever present, as are all the stops on my long journey to the NBA:

The years in England with five different teams, where it's said that no one cares about basketball, but I sure as hell did.

The college job where I found out I didn't yet know how to communicate with players—and that I better learn if I wanted a future in coaching.

The time I got fired from a good gig in Belgium by an impatient owner known to all as "Mr. V."

The three games I got to coach a forty-four-year-old Dennis Rodman.

My tour of duty in the D-League, including the season I had my Thanksgiving dinner at a Denny's in Sioux Falls, South Dakota.

I carry it all forward. Every crazy, maddening, fulfilling day of that three-decade odyssey.

Every championship—even the one that was followed by my star player heaving the Waterford crystal trophy in the direction of our owner and shattering it in a thousand pieces.

Every player I helped move on to a higher level.

Every moment that edged me closer to an NBA sideline.

Every bit of learning, every failure, and every success that propelled me to becoming coach of the Toronto Raptors—and to the night of June 13, 2019, when we defeated the Golden State Warriors and stood atop the pinnacle of the basketball world.

What you will read about in the pages that follow is the story of a quest, one that took me across national boundaries and from city to city and team to team in search of better opportunities—or sometimes just a job.

Over the span of more than a quarter century, I taught myself to organize and lead teams, to understand what motivates players, to draw up plays, to win more close games than I lost. I would come to know when my methods were failing and how to self-correct. I would think deeply about how I had been coached and even how I was parented—and I'd keep what I believed had value and reject a lot of the rest.

I found time to pick up a master's degree and am closing in on a PhD. Someone was quoted recently as saying I am a concert-level pianist, which is absurd. I'm not even close, but I'm not terrible, and on my off-hours on the road, I am just as likely to be playing jazz or blues on the keyboard I travel with as I am to be watching basketball tape.

I was never a part of any "coaching tree"—not a former assistant or disciple of Dean Smith, Gregg Popovich, Pat Riley, or any other basketball deity. I was a long way from all of that, a hoops vagabond, toiling in the basketball backwaters. In all honesty, it was lonely at times, and often difficult. I moved around a lot and from a certain perspective I'm sure it could look like I was going sideways, not up.

Some of the moves I had made probably did not seem explicable at the time, and perhaps do not even now. They were unorthodox, in part driven by a young man's yearning to see the world beyond a horizon of corn and soybean fields.

The last team in England I coached was the Brighton Bears, and I also owned them. It went horribly. When I finally came back home after that experience, after a dozen years of coaching overseas, I was out of money. And by that, I mean flat-out broke—the kind of broke where you move in with your sister and rent a P.O. box at a grocery store.

I wanted to write this book because I know the vast majority of people with aspirations of reaching some big goal are just like I was. They start out with no guarantees, no step-by-step route, probably not even a fully visible path.

They take a couple of steps forward and then get knocked back. I'm thinking about anyone trying to start a business—about the musician putting her stuff up on YouTube and trying to get noticed—or the kid from humble means driving an Uber at night while he tries to fight his way through college.

The point I hope that readers will take from what I've written is that it's not about the dream. It's about the work.

You put in the time and the sweat for the satisfaction of knowing you've thrown yourself into the struggle. And you do it to make sure that if somebody does give you that opportunity you were dreaming about, you're worthy of it.

1

CARROLL, IOWA

A FOUNDATION BUILT UP FROM A POLE-VAULT PIT

With my parents and eight siblings. (I'm the one on my mother's lap.)

(Nurse family collection)

Where does anyone begin when writing about how they grew up, their hometown, who raised them, and how? What felt important at the time but really wasn't, as opposed to what carries forward and sets your course in life? It's a lot of ground to cover, and hard to know what to assign value.

Random as it may seem, the first thing that feels relevant for me to pass along is that we had a pole-vault pit in our backyard. I think one of my older brothers talked his track and field coach into letting him bring a pole home after the high school season was over. It was before they were made of fiberglass, so our pole was bamboo or some other kind of flexible wood.

We dug the pit by loosening up the ground with shovels and spades and emptying bags of sand over the dirt. Then we threw a couple of old mattresses down and finished off the landing area with piles of old clothes. The crossbar hung between planks of wood with nails sticking out every six inches, so it could be raised or lowered to various heights.

I'm sure my father must have supervised the construction, but once the thing was built, my memories are of my brothers and me out there with other kids from the neighborhood, often five or six of us at a time, with no adults around. We'd make a big run, stick the pole in the ground, try to clear the bar, and hope it didn't hurt too much when we came back down.

Pole vaulting was one of those things, one of many, that we figured we could learn pretty much on our own if we put our minds to it. One Nurse boy passed it down to the next.

We also had these funny old instructional books with drawings of upper-body exercises and handstands and all this other stuff to do to make you a better pole vaulter. We did the exercises religiously, convinced that if we just applied ourselves like the book said, we'd become champion pole vaulters. We survived some broken bones and a lot of close calls.

My brother Dan set the pole vaulting record at our high school, Kuemper Catholic. Then my brother Tom broke it. When I got to high school, I broke Tom's record, clearing the bar at twelve feet, ten inches. That's still the record and I'm confident it will stand because Iowa high schoolers no longer compete in the pole vault. It was deemed too dangerous, along with the hammer throw and javelin.

I'd like to claim that I am the only NBA figure of any significance to have been a pole vaulter, but I'm enough of a basketball geek to happen to know that Tex Winter, Phil Jackson's old assistant coach and the architect of the triangle offense, was a world-class pole vaulter and would have been in the 1944 Olympics if they had not been canceled because of World War II.

My schooling, family life, pole vaulting, and just about all else of any importance in the first eighteen years of my life took place in or around Carroll, Iowa, which is roughly a hundred miles northwest of Des Moines, hard by the Middle Raccoon River. Carroll is in the opposite direction of Chicago, toward the corner of the state bordered by Minnesota, South Dakota, and Nebraska.

My mother was raised a short distance away, on a farm that is still in our family, though the farmhouse is gone. Her grandparents were homesteaders who came down from Ontario,

Canada. We spent a lot of time on the farm as kids among the crops, cows, and hogs—fishing in a good-sized pond formed by a creek that had been dammed up, and running around and inventing our own games.

My mom went to the same college I did, the University of Northern Iowa, but back when it was called the Iowa State Teachers College. She started teaching in a one-room schoolhouse and then for a long time was a substitute teacher in Carroll, working whatever days she could.

She did not have her first child until she was thirty-one, and she was forty-three when she had her ninth, which was me. I don't think she and my dad wasted a lot of undue time trying to think up inventive names for any of us. In addition to Tom and Dan, my other brothers are Jim, Ken, and Steve. My sisters got the names Susan, Michelle, and Maureen.

My dad was from Carroll proper, which with its ten thousand residents is the population center of an otherwise rural area and is sometimes referred to as the Big Apple. After serving in the navy during World War II, he went off to the University of Illinois and then came back to work as a mail carrier. For most of my childhood, he was our town's postmaster, and on weekends, he ran his own painting business.

Our house was small considering all the people living in it— just three bedrooms upstairs and one downstairs in the basement, where I slept, with a bunk bed and a couple of twins. One of the nonnegotiable things in the family was church. You went, no questions asked.

The whole area, pretty much, was Irish and German Catholic. (The town is named for Charles Carroll, the only Catholic with his signature on the Declaration of Independence.) We were about five blocks away from our parish church, and on Sunday mornings, the Nurse family filed into the pews, arriving in stages, depending on how fast any of us ate breakfast and got dressed.

On our free days during the summer, the rule was you did not leave the house until nine-thirty A.M. After that, you went out on your bicycle, usually somewhere to play ball with friends; returned promptly by twelve-thirty for lunch; rested for at least an hour (another ironclad rule); went back out; and came back for dinner at five-thirty. My mother had no idea where we were but Carroll was a place you didn't lock your doors or worry about too much.

When we got older, the expectation was that you worked. If you intended to go to college, you earned money toward it because there was no way a postmaster and a substitute teacher were paying tuition for nine kids. By my mid-teens, I was baling hay in the summers and "walking beans," as it's called—which means walking along rows of soybean with a hoe and digging out weeds that competed with the crop for water and nutrients.

The most lucrative of the farmwork we did was also the most difficult and unpleasant: detasseling corn. It was seed corn, meant to feed cattle—planted in two male rows and four female rows. The female row has a tassel on the top that has to be taken off so it can get pollinated. The corn would be six or seven feet tall, but the tassel hung down a little so you could reach it if you weren't tall enough. Or you bent the stalk a little bit to get it to your height.

In the hottest weeks of the summer, every boy I knew de-tasseled corn. The rows were at least a half-mile long. You walked up one row, came down another, stopped briefly for a drink of water, and then got started on a new row. You packed a lunch and ate it in about five minutes because you got paid according to how much ground you covered.

From what I hear, Iowa kids are not doing this work anymore. They don't want to. Their parents do not want them to. Migrants get it done.

The corn could easily cut you. Even if it was 95 degrees (and it often was) you dressed in jeans, a long-sleeve shirt, a bandana around your neck and socks on your hands—with little holes cut out for your fingers and pulled high on your forearms so your wrists didn't get sliced up.

If you were experienced at it, like my older brothers were, you got contacted directly by farms to come and work. I went out with them sometimes. Other times, I'd go to the steps of the courthouse with a couple of friends—one of my parents would drop me off at six A.M.—and we'd jump on one of the buses that came by. It dropped you off at a field, a crew boss pointed you in a direction of your rows, and you jumped off and went to work.

⌃

In addition to the compulsories of church, education, and work, the overriding theme in my family was sports, and that goes back to my dad. He was a big solid guy, about six foot three, a good athlete in his day, hardworking and stone-cold honest. In contrast to my mom—who always had a smile on her face—there was not a lot of back-and-forth with him. If he had something to say, it was probably to kick your ass about some chore you didn't do. He did his work, read every newspaper and magazine he could get his hands on, and listened to the Cubs on the radio. We used to say that if we could buy him anything, it would be patience.

Most of his waking hours were devoted to his regular job and the weekend work he did so he could keep our large household in food and clothes. But he also found time to basically serve as our town's sports czar.

He founded the local Little League and was its president for many years, and he organized big basketball tournaments for seventh and eighth graders. A couple of times a year, the local gyms would be packed with players and parents from all over the state. The events were sponsored by the Catholic Youth Organization (widely known as the CYO) but they were precursors of today's big AAU tournaments.

My dad coached a lot of my brothers' teams, though by the time I came along he was mostly just running the leagues and tournaments. I was the second baseman for Kuemper's baseball team, the point guard for the basketball team, and the fourth Nurse brother to be the starting quarterback for the varsity football team. It probably would have been all six of us except that there were times when we were in high school at the same time, so one of my brothers had to become a receiver and another was a lineman.

It was not clear to me for a long time what my best sport was, or even my favorite one, and I thought I might go to college to play baseball or football. I got a couple of scholarship offers to play quarterback at Division II schools before anyone expressed interest in me for basketball. But fate intervened. In my senior year at Kuemper, our basketball team set off on this miracle run through the state playoffs and it sort of clarified things by making basketball the one sport I couldn't imagine giving up.

⌃

Kuemper Catholic drew from fifteen little towns and farming hamlets all around Carroll—some of them just crossroads with a feed store, a grocery, a gas station, and maybe a John Deere dealership somewhere nearby. We played solid basketball but usually were no match for the city kids from Des Moines, Cedar Rapids, Sioux City, and some of the state's other urban areas.

Our coach was a gentleman of the old school, a man named Wayne Chandlee. If you were on the team or aspiring to be on it, you encountered him as a freshman because he taught a first-period class that was really a basketball practice. He came in each morning, blew a whistle, and the group formed into two lines.

For several minutes, we practiced shooting without a ball in our hands—just pantomimed the flick of the wrist and the follow-through as if we were shooting the ball toward the front of the rim. Then he would finally hand out basketballs, and you shot it—not at the rim—but just floated it at your partner in the other line in order to lock in the proper form. This went on for a long time.

I was still really scrawny when I first got to Kuemper and I started my shot at my hip, just to get the ball to the rim. But as I added strength and paid attention to the mechanics that Coach Chandlee was teaching, I got to be a pretty good shooter. It was one of my first important lessons in basketball, and an enduring one, right up until the present, in my job as coach of the Toronto Raptors: if you can shoot, there's a use for you.

The three-point line had just been instituted, but like most teams back then, at any level, we did not attempt many. A shot from beyond the arc was still considered a gimmick. You only took a large number of them if you were behind late in a game. We walked the ball up the floor and punched it inside to our post players.

I shot a high percentage of mostly midrange shots—but a low

volume. I remember one day in my junior year, after I had scored maybe twelve points in a game the night before, Coach Chandlee came up to me at a practice. I thought maybe he was going to compliment me, but instead, he said something like, "Nice game, but you need to calm it down a little."

It was obvious from the start of my senior season that our team was a little better than usual, but I don't think too many people considered us serious contenders to win a state title. We were never one of the schools on that list.

We lost a couple of games early on but then rattled off sixteen straight wins at the end of the regular season. After four playoff wins, we were on a tear of twenty straight victories going into the state final in March of 1985.

We had talent on our roster and also some size. Our center was Brian David, who was six foot nine and would go on to play at Arizona for Lute Olson, although he would only ever start a handful of games. Another of our bench players, Frank Molak, ended up as a starter at a Division I school, the University of Missouri, Kansas City—and I'd go on to be a four-year starter at Northern Iowa.

We got all the way to the state final game and were matched up against a high school called Waterloo West, which had already soundly defeated the tournament favorite. In contrast to the guys on our team who sort of eked their way onto Division I rosters, they had a kid who became a four-year starter at Iowa State and another who set the career scoring mark at the University of Hawaii.

They kind of blew our doors off right from the start, and by the end of the first quarter we were in danger of losing touch. We were down eight points early on, but it felt like more, and we were not the type of team that was going to come back from a huge deficit. The whole night had the feel of the movie *Hoosiers* (which came out the year after and was based on the true story of an underdog team from a small town in Indiana).

In the movie, Gene Hackman, the coach, says to his team after they start the same way we did, "Maybe we don't belong here!" Coach Chandlee was less dramatic. (It was, after all, a real game and not a movie.) He told us to trust one another, pass the ball to the open man, and help out on defense just like we had all year. I recall him saying, "You guys are just all worrying about yourselves."

Veterans Memorial Auditorium in Des Moines was packed to its eleven thousand capacity—with about five thousand of the fans having come from Carroll. The joke was that the entire town was there and the last one to leave for Des Moines was told to turn the lights out.

We settled down, got hold of ourselves, and started to slowly crawl back. We were down just four points at halftime, and then tied, 57–57, at the end of the third quarter. At that point, we had not attempted a single foul shot; they had shot seventeen of them but made just ten. I'm sure our fans were complaining about the officiating, but they drove the ball to the hoop more than we did and we probably legitimately committed most of the fouls that were called.

In the fourth quarter, we began to methodically build a lead. We were executing our offense, getting unbelievable shots, and guarding the hell out of them. After we got a comfortable lead, we went into a delay game. We were in deep foul trouble—I had four, and so did two of our other players—so it made sense to shorten the game.

There was no shot clock in Iowa high school basketball and still isn't. The state is proudly retro. We shot at those old fan-shaped backboards, which Iowa high school basketball still uses. When we got fouled and finally went to the line, we hit our shots.

By the end of the night, we had captured Kuemper's first and, to this day, only state basketball championship, with a 69–58 victory. I scored just six of those points, on two field goals and a couple of foul shots.

Waterloo West had a fierce full-court press that produced turn-overs and points for them, and my most critical job had been to calmly take care of the basketball and find open teammates so that we did not get overwhelmed by their pressure. After the game, their coach noted that we had "some smart, good ball-handling people out front" and singled me out for praise: "That Nurse, I can't say enough about him."

That was sort of my playing career in a nutshell. I was the proverbial "coach on the floor" whom opposing coaches tended to notice. Most of us coaches can see ourselves in these types—not the most physically gifted guy on the floor, but clever.

⌃

I think that all coaches, whether we are conscious of it or not, carry a part of our youth and high school coaches forward. Parts of them stay embedded within us forever.

Those first experiences set in your mind what a coach is. You come to understand what works for you and inspires your best performance—and what shuts you down and makes you play worse. (A coach can have either of those effects.) If you care deeply about sports, the coach looms large. There's a good chance he's the biggest figure in your life other than your parents.

Wayne Chandlee could be a real hardass, like just about any authority figure back then. When we came to the locker room at halftime of the state final game, I figured, *Oh, God, he's really going to lay into us.* We had not lost a game in a couple of months and were rarely behind. The few times we were getting beat, it was by lesser competition, and he'd let us know he wasn't happy.

But in the locker room that night, he barely raised his voice. He told us things were looking good. "You guys are doing a hell of a job," he said. "We've got this going in the right direction."

After our victory, he explained his approach to the sportswriters from around the state who had covered the game. Waterloo was a lot faster, he said, so we needed to "overcome speed with patience."

Someone asked him later about how he was able to get us to come out of the locker room in the second half and play with such poise. "We were super tight, and we were so afraid of making mistakes that we made them just for that reason," he said. "Our mistakes were coming by trying not to make mistakes."

Those comments are like a textbook guide for any coach trying to help a team through a pressure situation. All athletes—at all levels—have anxiety. The guys I coach now may look to fans like they've got the world by the tail, but believe me, they've got anxieties. A bundle of them.

Our high school coach took stock of our emotions and figured out what we needed at that moment. He was able to find his own sense of calm and sort of hand it over to us. That may seem like the most obvious thing in the world to do but it's really hard, and it took me a while to learn.

⌃

Another of Wayne Chandlee's lifelong gifts to his players was that he engaged our intellects and made it clear that one of the ways to get better as an athlete (or better, really, at anything) is by cracking a book. This was not merely a recommendation. He gave us required reading and weekly quizzes. He put in my mind that there are deep layers of knowledge in sports, wisdom that goes all the way back to the beginnings and as deep down as you want to explore.

If you looked at my career now—to some of the innovative things we've done in Toronto, to what was referred to as a "basketball laboratory" when I was coaching the Rio Grande Valley Vipers in the D-League, to some things from back in England nobody even knows about—you would probably categorize me as an innovator. A "disrupter," to use the current term.

And it's true, in its way. I've embraced new ways of doing things, but all of my ideas and methods are built out from a traditional foundation.

The game of basketball, on one level, is as simple as it could possibly be—ten players, round ball, ninety-foot-long hardwood court, a couple of hoops on either end. If you sat someone courtside who had never seen a game before, they would pick it up fairly quickly, as opposed to baseball or football, which take a long time to grasp even the basic rules.

Basketball is straightforward enough that you can trace its present all the way back to its origins. I saw a neat thing on Yahoo Sports, a sort of four degrees of hoops separation: James Naismith, who nailed the peach baskets on the walls at the Springfield, Massachusetts, YMCA in 1891 and wrote the "13 basic rules of 'Basket Ball,'" coached Phog Allen at the University of Kansas from 1905 to 1907. Allen coached Dean Smith at Kansas from 1949 to 1953. Smith coached Larry Brown at North Carolina from 1961 to 1963. Gregg Popovich, who has won five NBA titles with the San Antonio Spurs, and whom I coach against now, worked as an assistant coach to Brown from 1988 to 1992.

If Naismith could see a game now, he would be amazed by the players' size, skill, and athleticism. He'd probably want to call traveling on every play, and he might want the music turned down at time-outs. But I don't think he'd have too much trouble recognizing the game he invented or following the action.

Through Wayne Chandlee, I can trace my own basketball education back a couple of generations. Foremost on my high school coach's reading list was a book titled *Stuff Good Players Should Know: Intelligent Basketball from A to Z,* by Dick DeVenzio, a former player at Duke who for many years operated a series of camps known as Point Guard College. There was a copy of it in the school library and Coach Chandlee put a little piece of paper in it each week with the sections we were supposed to study.

If you looked at *Stuff Good Players Should Know,* which was first published in 1983, I'm pretty sure there are parts that would make you laugh—starting with the illustrations, which resemble those antiquated drawings from the old high school health texts. (A player in an illustration on how to box out for a rebound is drawn with his hands high and his palms facing out, like he's being held up at gunpoint.)

Some of the chapter titles are funny. In one called "Don't Be Stupid," he writes, "The concepts in this book are generally acceptable to coaches [but] if your coach disagrees on some particular point, don't be stupid and argue with him. *Do it his way.*"

There is also a chapter titled "POOP"—which is an acronym for "Pivot Out of Pressure." The advice in this passage is like nearly everything else in the book: commonsense hoops guidance. Just about every word of it is as applicable now as when he wrote it, and some of it might even be more relevant.

If you watch an NBA game, you'll notice that the referees do not allow defenders to touch the point guards. These guys are super-fast and skilled, and you can't impede them. You can barely breathe on them. This is one reason why it's become a point guard league.

However, once a point guard picks up his dribble—or any player on the floor does—you can basically butcher him. Just whack away at the ball and if you hit skin or bone on any part of the body (other than probably the head), you're good. No foul.

So what is an offensive player to do who is under this kind of assault? The highly detailed instruction DeVenzio gives to players who have picked up their dribble is one I'd still want my players to follow: "Twist your upper body a quarter turn to the side and then bring the ball down to your waist... You put your body between the defender and the ball, and you put your elbow in his face as you lower yourself into a crouch... The elbow in his face is not meant to hurt him, but its presence certainly keeps him from sticking his nose too close in case he is getting any ideas about going for a steal."

DeVenzio died very young, at fifty-two. He was way ahead of his time in many respects, including in his off-the-court opinions. One of his six other books, *Rip-Off U: The Annual Theft and Exploitation of Revenue Producing Major College Student-Athletes,* came out decades before most people were thinking about some of the inequities of the NCAA.

DeVenzio has other fans among modern coaches. Larry Brown, the only coach to have won an NCAA and NBA title, has referred to *Stuff Good Players Should Know* as a "sacred text" and the "Rosetta Stone" of the game.

It remains the best book ever written specifically for players, with advice ranging from what kind of pass to throw on a two-on-one fast break (nothing fancy; you're just as likely to fool your teammate as the other team), when to throw a bounce pass (rarely, because they take longer to reach their target), and how to set a screen (imagine your belt buckle against your opponent).

His book is still a go-to for me and I always find things in it to pass along. After I was named the Toronto Raptors head coach, I bought copies in bulk and handed them out to every player on the team. I have not, however, assigned my NBA players specific chapters to read—or hit them with any pop quizzes.

2

YOU ARE *NOT* GOING TO ITHACA, NEW YORK

MY FATHER'S VOICE, ECHOING THROUGH TIME

At the University of Northern Iowa being guarded by Tony
Bennett of the University of Wisconsin–Green Bay, the future
coach of the University of Virginia. *(Courtesy of the University
of Northern Iowa)*

Early in my senior year at Kuemper Catholic, I started getting letters from the basketball coaches at Cornell. They had seen me at a camp that summer in Rensselaer, Indiana, where I thought I had played well, but Cornell was the only school I heard from.

That January, I got a call from their head coach. The phone in our living room was planted between my dad's La-Z-Boy recliner and another big chair my mom liked to sit in. I talked to the coach, Tom Miller, while my dad "read" the newspaper, though I knew he was listening to every word I said.

"Thank you very much for calling," I said before hanging up the phone.

"Who was that?" my dad asked.

"It was the coach at Cornell University in Ithaca, New York. He wants me to play for them and wants me to come out for a visit right away."

"You are *not* going to Ithaca, New York," my dad said, and then went right back to reading his newspaper.

It's been more than thirty years since this happened, and over that time, I've told this story to a few people. They always ask, "What did you say to your dad after that?"

Here's the amazing thing: I didn't say anything. I didn't even ask him why he didn't want me to go to Cornell, and to this day, I don't know why.

Back in those days, you were scared of your father. Or at least a lot of the kids I knew were. Maybe it was a little more true in my part of the country. With my dad, it was never a dialogue. Whatever he said was the last word.

Cornell continued to write letters and they kept calling. I think they may have missed on some prospects they wanted, and they really stepped it up with me. But I didn't bring it up again with my father.

I let it drop when I realized it was not going to happen. But it put an idea in my head that there was more out there, and it also gave me a lifelong, self-diagnosed case of "Ivy League envy"—a question in my head if I could have made it as an athlete and student at an Ivy League school. I'm sure that it is what led me, years later, to pursue graduate studies at the Harvard Extension School.

The other thing it did was help make clear to me that once I left the house, I would own my decisions. In a different way, it was like being out in the backyard with the pole-vaulting pole in your hands. You get over the bar or you don't. It's on you.

That was part of what gave me the courage and conviction to coach overseas and chart an unconventional path. At twenty-some years old, I was not going to begin going back to my dad and asking, "What do you think?" because we had never had that kind of two-way conversations and I wasn't about to start then.

^

I'd never say that Iowa is the best place on earth to live or to raise children. I've lived in too many parts of the country and world to believe that any place has that particular claim. But it was good for me. And it was also good to leave.

Our parents, in a sense, are our first coaches—our first teachers and authority figures. I think to be a successful person, let alone a successful coach, it helps to be conscious of what inclinations you carry forward from your parents. You want to keep the best parts of them and eliminate the others.

My mom was super talkative, super nice, always wanted to know what was on your mind. She was a teacher at heart. I try to coach with a little joy in my bones and a smile on my face, and that comes from her.

With my dad, it's more complicated. I think I have his work ethic and integrity, and I can be as direct as I need to be, which I probably learned from him. And believe me, it's useful.

In my Raptors office, I have an elephant on my desk. My assistant, Geni Melville, picked it up on the street in Toronto. It's made of some kind of bronze and is the so-called elephant in the room—a visual reminder of the need to have hard conversations and face things head-on.

Say I have a player in my office who wants more minutes, but he doesn't shoot a high enough percentage to help us when he's out there. He takes too many difficult shots, stops the offense because he doesn't move the ball, doesn't pass it.

Well, say hi to the elephant. I have to say to him: You want to get on the floor? You want to get paid? This is what you have to do.

I'm not doing the team or this guy any good if I sugarcoat it just to make him feel better. If I do that, he goes back out there and does the same dumb stuff, we probably lose a game, and he ends up back on the bench.

I've been around coaches who do not want to have the hard conversations. What happens is the problem mushrooms. If you get an injury or two and need the player and he screws up again—which he will definitely do if you didn't try to change him—you end up with a bunch of other guys pissed off that you didn't coach him properly. You started off with one problem and now you have ten.

The important thing is when I have my elephant-in-the-room moment, I don't want it to be a one-way conversation. That's a big thing I learned from my upbringing. I don't want to be the only one in the room talking.

When the other person has his say, there's a good chance I'll learn something. Maybe I'm giving him the wrong prompts. I'm telling him one thing but he's hearing something else.

There's no way that I could coach in the modern NBA with my father's my-way-or-the-highway approach, nor would I want to. I am not my players' boss in a traditional sense. For one thing, even some end-of-the-bench guys make more money than I do (and I'm very well paid by any normal standard) and a couple of the stars literally make ten times my salary.

But even if I was their boss, I'd want to hear their views—and probably especially when they disagree with me. The NBA has moved in that direction. The world has.

^

I've gone after jobs I desperately wanted and could not even get an interview, and when I look back, I was lucky. A lot of those jobs would have been dead ends. I tried really hard to get a job at Drake University. I once accepted a job as an assistant at Iowa State and then quickly changed directions when the head coach who hired me, my old teammate at Northern Iowa, Greg McDermott, moved on to Creighton. Those might have been good jobs, but I don't know that either of them would have led to the NBA.

In the same way, I have no way of knowing how my life would have been different if I'd gone to Cornell. I might have ended up on Wall Street and made tons of money and despite my wealth, been miserable as hell. I might, somehow, have found my way into the NBA through some alternative series of twists and turns, though that doesn't seem all that likely.

What got me to Northern Iowa was some luck that came my way—and as is often the case in sports, my good fortune was someone else's misfortune. After we won the high school championship, I got chosen for our state's high school all-star event, which was called the Dr Pepper Classic.

I was not slated to start and I'm not sure how much I would have played. The starting point guard on our South squad was going to be a kid named Eddie Conroy, a really good player who was first team, all-state. He had already agreed to play for the Citadel, the college that may be best known from the books written by his cousin, the late novelist Pat Conroy. (Eddie, who is still a good friend, became head coach at Citadel and Tulane and is now an assistant at the University of Minnesota.)

I was playing second base and pitching for our high school baseball team at this point. I still didn't know where I was going to college and what, if any, sport I would play. In a practice the night before the Dr Pepper Classic, Eddie cracked a rib and I stepped into his starting role.

I'm sure I was thinking that this was my last chance to show myself to college coaches, and that can go two ways: it can inspire you to play really well or cause you to throw up a bunch of bad shots and try to do stuff you're not capable of. But I kind of went bonkers in the game. Scored a bunch of points, dished out assists.

The game was played in Cedar Falls at the arena on Northern

Iowa's campus. When it was over, the coach there at the time, Jim Berry, came down and said, "You can play here." He offered me a scholarship, and I said, right on the spot, "I'll take it."

Two big things happened to me at Northern Iowa that influenced my career. One was that I was exposed, for the first time, to a team that did not cohere. It was just a bad experience that first season, and if you're a future coach, it's probably not the worst thing to see what that looks like. As painful as it may be, you experience, firsthand, what you do not want to create.

I started a dozen games and was the only first-year player to get real playing time. I wish I could say I was welcomed by the older guys, but there wasn't a whole lot of camaraderie going around in any direction. It felt like there was a fistfight every other day in practice.

In some other sports, I'm not sure how much it matters if guys get along. If you've got a left fielder on a big-league team who hits fifty home runs and he's a selfish jerk, he circles the bases, gets his high-fives, and sits back down in the dugout by himself. Your spot in the lineup comes around and you get your swings no matter what kind of mood he's in. You don't need him to pass you the ball.

Basketball relies on a lot of little human interactions. There might be as many as ten passes that lead to one basket. On defense, you constantly help your teammates—if one loses his man, you leave your guy and cover his; if the ball swings back to the guy you just left, another teammate covers for you.

If you are sitting courtside at a basketball game, you'll hear players shouting out switches as they play this "help" defense. A quiet team is in almost all cases a losing team. A basketball team does not have to be composed of players who are best friends, but it never works if they don't like and trust one another.

About halfway through my freshman season at Northern Iowa, we lost a really close game to St. Francis College of Illinois, 70–68. We were Division I, a so-called mid-major that had never made the NCAA tournament; they were an NAIA team. (The National Association of Intercollegiate Athletics is a much smaller competitor of the NCAA and, generally speaking, composed of less-competitive teams.) It was one of those gut-wrenching games where you look back and can't figure out how you possibly lost.

The defeat was the last straw for our coach. With our record standing at 4-6 and more than half the season left to play, he announced before the next practice that he would be stepping down at the end of the season. From his quotes in the local paper, the *Waterloo Courier*, it seemed like he had been thinking about it for a while. "I've had this in the back of my mind for a couple of years," he said. "I've talked it over with my family...On my way to work Thursday morning—while I was driving in my car—it was like something hit me on the head. The thought came to me to get out now. I have no desire to coach right now. I've been doing it twenty-six years and it gets old."

We were all shocked by his announcement, and it was certainly a strange way to start out my college career to find out that my coach was so unhappy in the job. It was not as bad as a parent walking out on a marriage, but you did feel a little responsible. You sort of wonder: What did I do? Did I cause this? The season did not get any better—we finished with a record of 8-19.

Coach Berry was a good basketball man with a deep love of the game who later coached again on the high school level in Iowa. The opportunity he gave me was not one that anyone else was offering. It's one of those moments where if he had not taken a chance on me, I have no idea where I would be right now.

⌃

The other big thing that happened at Northern Iowa was purely positive. Throughout my playing career, going back to high school—and all through my coaching career—the art of shooting a basketball with proper form has been a major theme. In high school, I learned Shooting 101 from Wayne Chandlee. After my freshman year of college, I was fortunate to fall into what amounted to a master class in shooting from Chris Mullin, an all-American at St. John's who was just starting his Hall of Fame NBA career. And then later that same summer, I encountered a coach named Des Flood, who was also known as Dr. Shot.

As to why shooting is so important, I will resort (with apologies in advance) to some corporate-sounding language: Any business ought to focus relentlessly on its core mission. If you manufacture candy, you probably should pay attention to the ingredients and the taste before you get too carried away with the wrapper. If you make cars, you don't start with the cupholders.

Shooting, obviously, is integral to the mission of any basketball team. You can't score and can't win without getting the ball in the basket. But a lot of fans would be shocked by how little time and thought, even in top college and professional settings, is devoted to shooting technique.

All that shooting instruction that Coach Chandlee gave us,

starting in those ninth grade, first-period classes—the miming of shots and the flicking of wrists without a ball in our hands— paid off in a state title. We had zero chance of competing against the state's better teams without our superior ability to shoot. For those of us who went on to play basketball in college, shooting is what gave us the opportunity.

One of our players, Roger Gehling, a six-foot-five kid who played at a junior college, went absolutely bananas in the state tournament. He made twenty-three of twenty-eight shots over the course of our three-game playoff run. For the tournament, our team converted on 60 percent of our field goal attempts— which is incredible at any level, let alone for a bunch of high school kids playing in front of more fans and under more pressure than they have ever faced.

Northern Iowa hosted a couple of basketball camps early in the summer, after classes ended, with the current players serving as counselors, and that's where I met Chris Mullin. He was a guest speaker and he took it really seriously. I would imagine that whoever was his shoe sponsor paid for his visit.

His big message was about footwork—being ready to shoot the ball before it's in your hands rather than catching it, pivoting in the direction of the basket, and then figuring out how to get a shot off.

There's more attention now to teaching and no shortage of instructional videos on the market. If you're a serious basketball player or have a kid who is one, you may have come across this information: get ready to shoot before the ball reaches you. But even some very good players do not do this effectively; instead, they want to catch the ball and then wait a beat before deciding what to do with it. Against a good defender, that's too late.

I knew as soon as I got to Northern Iowa that it was a big jump for me and I better get in the gym if I wanted to keep my scholarship. There was a reason I was not being recruited on that level. Everybody was bigger, stronger, and faster. I did what I could to improve myself athletically—added some muscle, tried to get faster—but Chris Mullin gave me a basketball solution.

He talked about getting "behind the ball" as it was being passed to you, with your knees bent, in order to rise up and release a shot before it could be defended. Even if I wasn't quick enough to get much separation from a defender, I could get a shot off quickly. These are the principles I still teach in the NBA.

I spent the rest of that summer in Iowa City lifting weights and practicing Mullin's techniques. (And also riding around on a 1974 Yamaha motorcycle.) I was playing in a summer league in Iowa City with some really good college players from the University of Iowa and Iowa State, and that's where I met Des Flood, who was Coach Tom Davis's shooting coach at Iowa at a time when shooting coaches were very rare.

I sort of attached myself to him. He gave me insights on concentration and holding my follow-through—keeping my wrist and fingers on my shooting hand pointed right at the rim until the ball went through the net.

It was in this time frame—an intense couple of months—that I really became a student of shooting. It was another lesson for me, one that I pass along to players, especially those who have the talent for an NBA career but are not stars: If you want to stay in basketball, devote yourself to shooting. If you're already a good shooter, become a better one.

It's the one skill in the game that nearly anyone can get better at. Take a look at Michael Jordan's career stats. When he came into the league, he shot very few three-point shots and his percentage on the ones he attempted was awful—under 20 percent in each of his first four seasons. He was such a dominant athlete that he did not need to shoot from distance.

As he lost some of his explosiveness, he practiced his outside shooting and he got better at it. In the season when he was thirty-two years old, he attempted 260 three-pointers—a healthy number, more than three a game—and connected on 43 percent, which is excellent.

I averaged only about four points a game in my first season at Northern Iowa. I never became a big scorer but in my last two seasons, armed with better fitness and the knowledge I gained from Chris Mullin and Des Flood, I scored almost ten a game. The team and the experience got a lot better. Under our new coach, Eldon Miller, we went 19-9 in my senior year.

Much more telling than the points I scored, in terms of my own career and the future direction of NBA basketball, is how I scored them. In my junior and senior seasons, I attempted 274 shots from beyond the three-point arc, connecting on 133 of them. I put up just ninety-nine shots from inside the arc and made fifty-two.

Basically, I attempted three-pointers and layups and virtually nothing in between. That shot pattern is an extreme version of what we installed with the Rio Grande Valley Vipers and what I teach now in Toronto—and it's what most coaches in the NBA now tell their players. Why take a tough two-pointer if you can take an open three-pointer or drive the ball to the basket and get a bucket or get fouled?

Back at Northern Iowa, I was not thinking about a system; I was just trying to survive. I knew I couldn't drive past guys or get shots up over them, so I gravitated to an open space where I would be less closely guarded and, by the way, get an extra point if I put the ball through the hoop.

⌃

3

LONDON CALLING

ALSO ON THE LINE: DERBY, BIRMINGHAM, MANCHESTER, AND BRIGHTON

With Ronnie Baker of the London Towers.

(Copyright © Ahmed Photos; photographs by Mansoor Ahmed/Ahmed Photos)

Basketball, as a lot of people know, is increasingly a global game. There were 108 international players in the NBA at the start of the 2019–20 season, nearly a quarter of the league's total. They were from thirty-eight countries. Eleven of them had made at least one NBA All-Star Game.

The influx of players from outside the US is not a new phenomenon, but there has been a steady upswing in both quantity and quality. Four of the five major individual awards in 2019 went to foreign-born players, which would have been unimaginable a couple of decades ago: MVP, Giannis Antetokounmpo (Greece); rookie of the year, Luka Dončić (Slovenia); defensive player of the year, Rudy Gobert (France); and most improved player, Pascal Siakam (Cameroon), who plays for me with the Raptors.

Numerous corners of the world are producing this talent: the traditional basketball hotbeds of Eastern and Western Europe; South America; Asia; and, increasingly, Africa, where the NBA has a great deal of effort and money to nurture players.

Canada is the richest source of non-US-born talent, with twenty players currently on NBA rosters. Two of them play for me with the Raptors—Chris Boucher and Oshae Brissett. Another Canadian, RJ Barrett, was the third overall pick in the 2019 NBA draft. Andrew Wiggins was the first overall pick in the 2014 draft. Several other Canadians—including Jamal Murray and Shai Gilgeous-Alexander—appear headed for stardom.

One reason I feel fortunate to coach in Toronto, the NBA's only non-US market, is that it's as good a basketball city as exists anywhere. Just under twenty thousand fans file in for every home game at Scotiabank Arena, and sometimes more with standing room. There hasn't been an empty seat in years—and it's loud.

I wrote about going over to Derby, England, after I left the University of Northern Iowa. That was my first experience in international basketball and my first (and much shorter) of two tours in England.

I stayed just one season before taking a job back in Iowa as the head coach at Grand View University, an NAIA school in Des Moines. I was twenty-three years old, the youngest coach across the whole NCAA, a boy wonder. And I had no idea what the hell I was doing.

It was the first time I tried to lead without also playing and I found out I wasn't very good at the essential mission of a coach: communicating what I wanted my players to do and getting them to do it. I coached them like I had been coached as a kid. When they didn't do what I wanted, I yelled. When that didn't work, I yelled more—but louder. I'm pretty sure the players were as confused and frustrated as I was.

After two years, I took an assistant's job at the University of South Dakota. It was an NCAA Division II school, and I wasn't the head coach, but it was important to my growth.

The town of Vermillion, South Dakota, is a slow-moving place. There was a nine-hole golf course that I used to play in the warmer months with my head coach, Dave Boots, and we'd go around and around—maybe four times for thirty-six holes, or we'd keep on going if we felt like it. I'd have my breakfasts at the

Cowboy restaurant—$3.99 for a man-sized pile of food. In the winter months it was routine for the temperature to fall below zero, and there was not a hell of a lot of daylight.

Those were the longest days of my life, and I mean that mostly in a good way. I had been knee-deep in the Xs and Os of basketball, all the tactical stuff, but I realized I had to devote myself to learning more about human behavior. My future was not going to be determined by being the coach who could draw up the most clever plays on a whiteboard.

And I wasn't going to be satisfied just doing that, either. I needed to connect better. I needed to know how to make teams come together around their common interests and really trust each other—the way any winning basketball team must do.

Having been humbled at Grand View, I began to study educational psychology. South Dakota was where I earned my master's degree. My academic advisor was a very smart man named Henryk Marcinkiewicz, whose field was educational psychology. It gnawed at me that I had not gotten through to my previous team, at Grand View, and I think I was still trying to figure out why.

I got interested in the questions of how different people learn. How do they take in information? How, as a teacher or coach, can you best make yourself understood? How do you motivate a team? How do you tap into players' self-interest and make clear that the closer they follow your directions, the better it will be for them?

I would later meet Art Safer, a professor of leadership at Concordia University in Chicago—where I'm currently studying for my PhD—who became both a mentor and a friend. I have certainly been driven by an intellectual curiosity about how to lead, but there's an obvious overlap with my profession.

As a coach, I needed to know what concise instruction looked like—the kind that come clear to a young athlete in the course of a ninety-minute practice or that can be conveyed in a sixty-second time-out.

⌃

When I went back to England for a second time in 1995—after my stint of college coaching in the US—I was not exactly entering the glorious new world of global basketball I described at the beginning of this chapter.

You could easily rattle off a couple dozen countries where the game was more popular. There are the obvious ones, like Germany, Croatia, Russia, France, Spain, Brazil, and Argentina, which were almost always competitive at the Olympics and world basketball championships and already had sent—or soon would send—players to the NBA. You would include Nigeria and the Democratic Republic of the Congo, the homelands of Hall of Famers Hakeem Olajuwon and Dikembe Mutombo. And China, Japan, South Korea, and just about every other nation in Asia, which were all becoming basketball crazed.

England, not so much.

The *Wall Street Journal* has written that basketball in the United Kingdom "isn't just a minor sport… compared to the likes of soccer, rugby and cricket—it may not even be as popular as snooker." You could probably add one more sport to that list—darts, which gets a lot of TV time over there.

But if I'm really going to take a clear, hard look at my career up to that point, I was not exactly working in the center lane of American basketball before I headed back overseas. Grand View was way off the radar. At South Dakota, I thought I did a good job as a recruiter, but I was an assistant coach, and while the school was a perennial Division II power and headed toward moving up to Division I, it wasn't there yet.

When I decided to go back to England, nobody wrote any stories that said *Nick Nurse was a shooting star in American basketball! What the hell is he doing?* Other than my family and friends, I'm not sure how many people knew I left.

I went back because I wanted to coach pros—at whatever level—and I wanted to run a team and make the decisions. I'm sure it may sound vain, but I think I have the makeup of a head coach and I've felt that way as far back as I can remember. I was that kid in the sixth grade who said, "Let's get a team together and try to beat the seventh graders."

Between 1995 and 2006, I put in probably seven hundred games as a head coach. I was the guy making the substitutions, calling the time-outs, talking at halftime, drawing up the end-of-game plays with the score tied. For most of that decade, I was coaching in England, but I ran teams over the summers at an NBA camp in Treviso, Italy, at the NBA Summer League in California, and just about anywhere else I could get a gig on a sideline.

I have people who ask me now how to get in the coaching business. A lot of the time, I think what they mean is: How can I enter as high up in the field as I can? And I get that. Everything's better at the upper levels, whether it's a good college job or just about anything in the NBA. The pay is better, the hotels, the status, the postgame spread.

What's not always better, if you're just the guy whispering suggestions in a head coach's ear, is the experience. I tell anyone who wants to rise up in the business to coach anywhere you can. Grab an AAU team. Coach a high school JV. If you're currently an assistant coach, find some place in the off-season where you're the guy who has to figure out a way to win.

When I took over the Birmingham Bullets in 1995, it was a big step up from my first go-round in England five years before. It was a bigger city than Derby. They were renovating the downtown, and the National Indoor Arena, where we played our games, was one of the big showpieces.

Our owner, Harry Wrublewski, was an Australian and a big-time promoter. I'd work alongside him in the mornings as we tried to figure out how to sell tickets, how to get us coverage on radio and TV, and how to make the team stay afloat financially. Then I would run a practice and come back to the office and work with Harry the rest of the day.

British basketball, at least to a degree, was on the upswing. The league was marketing itself as family-friendly entertainment—a sport that avoids "the hooliganism that blights soccer," as the *New York Times* put it. Tickets were affordable and the league was getting some television viewership after signing a contract with Sky TV.

Players still were not paid much. Each team had a salary cap of something like $100,000—less than a couple of the NBA's top stars, at that point, made for a single game. My salary was about $300 a week, plus an apartment and a car.

I didn't care very much. I was still only twenty-seven years old, though at six years into my career, I wasn't a rookie coach anymore. But if I had been driven by money, I would have already used my accounting degree to get a proper job or figured out some other way to make a living.

What did bother me in Birmingham was the team's losing culture, which everyone seemed to take for granted. We started out the year alternating wins and losses, and some of the losses were just senseless—games that would have been victories with just one halfway intelligent play down the stretch.

The coup de grâce came about six weeks into the season. We were down one point with about six seconds left and our player was on the line with two free throws.

He made the first and tied it up. He missed the second. My guy grabbed the rebound, dribbled it to half-court, and threw it up in the air, celebrating the "win."

Everybody in the arena was looking at him, thinking, *You idiot. It's a tie game.*

I had these two stats guys sitting next to me and one of them turned my way and said, "Typical Birmingham Bullets basketball. We've been doing it for twenty years."

I don't know, maybe that was supposed to console me. You know, *Poor bloke, just another coach who's going to have to endure this shit until he can find something better to do. Let's go out later and have a pint and forget it all.*

That was not my response. We went on to lose in overtime. (Of course.) I went home that night and I thought, this whole place needs a fucking makeover. And then I wrote out, on Birmingham Bullets letterhead, three words in big capital letters: EXPECT TO WIN.

I wrote a little letter under it and went to the office the next day and made a bunch of copies and handed them out to everybody in the organization, not just the players. And it made a big difference, because it changed the whole organization's mindset.

In the letter, I wrote: "When you come here every night, when you come to the arena, whether you're a volunteer or a ticket-taker or a stat guy, you need to get on board with providing the energy that we're going to win tonight."

Was this an amazingly brilliant thing to do? Not really. It was blunt and a little corny, but sometimes that's what you do as a coach. You're dealing with young athletes—you have to hit them over the head with the obvious. You invest everybody around them in their success because it actually helps them. They need that lift.

My time in Birmingham, where I went after South Dakota, marked the beginning of many years, still ongoing, of what in education circles is sometimes called self-directed learning. I was hungry for knowledge and a sponge for anything having to do with basketball, coaching, and leadership.

But I was also on my own—on an island (literally) that did not have much to offer in the way of accumulated basketball wisdom. The people who might otherwise have been my mentors, and possibly my sponsors for jobs up the coaching ladder in the US, were across an ocean, thousands of miles away.

It was rare to see American basketball on television. Maybe they'd show some of the NBA Finals, live, which meant it came on at three in the morning. But a company in Germany shipped VHS cassettes with broadcasts of recent NBA games, with at least two games on each tape. Every Friday I'd get my shipment of three tapes. (I paid nine or ten pounds for them, or about fifteen bucks, so considering what I was making they weren't cheap.)

I'd binge-watch them as soon as they arrived and then play them for the team before or after practices and on the bus as we traveled to away games. (That was another upgrade from Derby—we had an actual bus rather than traveling in a van.) Sometimes a few of us would get together in a pub that was attached to our arena and watch there. By the time the next shipment arrived, I'd seen each of the games multiple times.

You could request specific games. This was when Phil Jackson was in the middle of his run of six NBA titles with the Chicago Bulls, and I ordered every one of their games. Like nearly every other basketball fan, I was captivated by those Bulls teams and, of course, the allure of their star, Michael Jordan.

What interested me the most, though, was Jackson's triangle offense. It had been brought to him by his assistant, Tex Winter. Another coach, Sam Barry, whom Winter played for at the University of Southern California, is sometimes credited as having instituted an early version of it. Whatever its lineage, Jackson and the Bulls refined it, expanded it, and perfected the triangle—and everything about it appealed to me.

The offense involves, first of all, generous spacing between the five offensive players. The center positions himself just outside the lane, usually on the high block (near the foul line), and he is one point of a triangle. Two perimeter players, both of them outside the three-point arc and on the same side of the court as the center, are the other two points. A fourth offensive player is at the top of the key, and the fifth is on the opposite side of the court (the weak side).

What people notice initially about this offense is its shape, what at first seem to be the fixed positions. The triangle is clear to see, even by a casual fan. But the real beauty of the triangle lies in its improvisational nature.

In response to how they read the defense, players have an almost infinite range of options. They can cut in various directions, execute pick-and-roll plays, or dribble handoffs—or they can feed the post, set picks for teammates, and basically exchange positions.

The triangle offense relies on intelligent players who can operate within a system that can seem contradictory. It puts them in what may look like a rigid, geometric structure, but at the same time gives free rein to their athleticism and imagination. The offense is meant to be continuous. Players do not reset and call a new play; they just flow to the next option.

Part of what I loved about the triangle was its beauty. It was basketball I liked to watch. All of us coaches who are successful are unnaturally competitive—or unhealthily so, depending on your perspective. I can get pretty worked up about designing a single inbounds play. I'll put a lot of time and thought into it with the hope that it will get me a couple of additional hoops over the course of an eighty-two-game season (more than one hundred with the playoffs) and if I'm lucky, maybe steal an extra victory.

Free-flowing basketball is often compared to jazz, and the triangle was, to my mind, the jazziest hoops I had ever seen. It was the opposite of what had been the norm—throw the ball to a big guy in the post, have him try to muscle up a basket, and if that doesn't work, ping it back out to the perimeter and start again.

Maybe it's partly a selfish thing on my part. Coaches get paid to win. It's how we keep our jobs—or get the next job. But if I'm going to coach a team, that means I have to watch them every game. It's not like I buy a ticket and need to be entertained, but even so, I don't enjoy looking at a static offense that just keeps pounding the ball in to the biggest guy on the court. I like something more aesthetically pleasing.

And it *is* entertainment in the end. We're trying to put people in the stands, whether the games are in England or Chicago. If at all possible, it's nice to put a fun product out there.

The triangle was the start of a revolution in basketball, a bridge to what you see in the NBA today: less emphasis on bulky centers who set up in the low post and more on versatile athletes who can play inside or outside. The game's top big men are still massive human beings, usually in the vicinity of seven feet, but most of the good ones are comfortable playing far from the basket and taking three-point shots. This style of play is sometimes called "positionless" basketball—or, when a team forgoes a center altogether and puts five normal-sized (by NBA standards) guys on the court, "small ball."

In Birmingham, my slogan ("Expect to Win") hit the mark and seemed to wake the team up. We started the regular season 8-8; we finished it with a record of 26-10.

I also got to act on my obsession with the Chicago Bulls offense. We did not have a Michael Jordan or a Scottie Pippen. We didn't even have a Bill Wennington or Luc Longley. But we did play the triangle—or our version of it.

Our biggest player was six foot seven. Just about the whole roster was the size of guards and small forwards. I'm known now as a coach who is willing to experiment. Earlier in my career, a lot of the experimentation was by necessity.

The triangle was the basis of our offense in Birmingham, but with so many undersized players on the court, our approach was an early example of small ball. When I was still a young player, coaches did not like to see us launch too many three-point shots. I had no such qualms.

I put guys all over the perimeter and encouraged them to fire away. It was the mid-1990s in England but our style, if you could ignore the quality of the players, looked a lot like the present-day NBA.

I didn't mind getting creative with defense, either. Our main rival that season was the London Towers. They were one of the rich teams in the league and for the last decade had won just about everything in sight.

I knew they were the team to beat. I lived out in the country but right off the motorway, and every chance I got, I'd jump in the car and drive the ninety miles to Wembley to scout them.

They had two really good players—Steve Bucknall, who had a solid college career at North Carolina and a very brief one (eighteen games with the Lakers) in the NBA. Bucknall and another good player, Danny Lewis, did just about everything for the Towers on offense, and everybody else got out of their way.

In the regular season, we played a defense against them that I called ZMT, which stood for zone, man, trap. We put one player each on Bucknall and Lewis, two in a zone, and one rover to trap whoever had the ball.

The guys playing man-to-man picked up the Towers' two stars full court and just face-guarded them, nose to nose, for the whole ninety feet. When they got winded, I'd put in two other defenders to take their places. I did this every two or three minutes, like hockey substitutions.

It was the kind of gimmick that a lot of people might think: Yeah, cool that you did that in England, but you'd never get away with it in the NBA. Well, maybe not *exactly* like that—definitely not the hockey substitutions and probably not the full-court face-guarding of a guy without the ball. But maybe something similar?

Years later, lots of stuff would come out of my memory bank and I'd put it into practice in NBA games—and sometimes at some very big moments.

One other big lesson I learned in Birmingham was to truly let players have a voice and lead. I had certainly benefited from that as an athlete. My football coach back at Kuemper Catholic, Mark Dalton, let me call my own plays as a high school quarterback, which was unusual, but I welcomed the opportunity because I felt like I was the one on the field and I knew what would work.

When I played point guard, in both high school and college, the coaches did not ask me to look to the bench before I called out an offensive set. When the clock was running, I was in charge.

We had defeated the London Towers in the regular season playing those junk defenses, as they are commonly known. We played the Towers again for the postseason championship, a one-game playoff. By British basketball standards, there was a big buzz, with our players getting pulled away the day before for TV and radio interviews. It was a big deal for our team and our fan base and lots of people traveled down to Wembley Arena for the game.

We had some good athletes on our squad, including Tony Dorsey, who had played on an NCAA Division II national champion at North Alabama University. Another of our top guys, Nigel Lloyd, was a tough-minded guard from Barbados who would play another decade in the British Basketball League (BBL), until he was forty-four years old. (He is second on the all-time-points list in Britain and first in career assists.)

When I look back at my time in England it's players like these whom I think about. People want to discredit British basketball, and I get it, but you could walk into any gym with Dorsey and Lloyd and know they would fight to win. For a coach learning his trade, they gave me plenty to work with, and the same goes for the other players I had over there.

In the pregame locker room, I said, "We're going to play the ZMT defense again. Concentrate on their two stars, take them out of the game, and let someone else try to beat us." My guys pushed back. They said no, we can guard them straight up, man-to-man.

I said fine. Go get 'em. They were fully invested in the strategy because they had, in essence, chosen it. We played solid but traditional team defense. If either Bucknall or Lewis beat their defender, someone came over and helped. But we did not go back to the junk defense.

We were in control all game and won it, 78–72. It was my first title since the one back at Kuemper Catholic.

4

AN AMERICAN ABROAD

MR. V WANTS TO SEE YOU. HURRY, HURRY!

After winning a championship with the
Manchester Giants in 2000.
(Copyright © Ahmed Photos; photographs by
Mansoor Ahmed / Ahmed Photos)

The championship I won in Birmingham—and whatever acclaim came out of quickly elevating a longtime losing franchise to the top—got me the opportunity to coach in Belgium with a club called Telindus Oostende. I wish I could tell you what I learned there. Maybe that sometimes shit just doesn't work out and you've got to put it behind you and move on.

The job was a significant career upgrade, and it was a big deal for me to land it. Dave Adkins, who I've been close with now for thirty-some years, helped get me the job. He had coached all over the world, including in Australia and Mozambique, before he became an agent.

Oostende had a history of being good, dominated the domestic league in Belgium just about every year, and was sometimes a force in the Euro League. I was coaching better players and making about $90,000 for the season, a 300 percent raise. Bonuses for wins pushed the potential salary to more than $100,000.

At a dinner for sponsors after I got hired, I gave a speech and said that I had been the youngest coach in the NCAA at Grand View, the youngest in England, and now the youngest in Belgium. (I was thirty.) Then I joked, I wonder how long I can keep this up?

In England, teams just picked up players where they could—whoever they could find locally, older guys coming over from Europe who were on the downside of their careers, whatever second- or third-tier prospects from the US that agents pitched them.

Like the other top basketball clubs in Europe, Oostende had an infrastructure and it operated on the same model as international soccer. They signed some seasoned players, not NBA quality but some who were not that far off. They brought in young prospects and coached them from their mid-teens on up. They had a first team that played in the league games, a second team made up of younger players who competed on another circuit, and a youth academy for even younger kids who showed promise.

The job was almost like a 9-to-5. We practiced in the mornings and then they fed the players right there at the practice site. If we didn't have a game that night, we practiced again in the afternoon.

The team was not ideally constructed. Its social fabric, to use that term, was a bit frayed—or to be more specific, it was ripped in three pieces. We had four guys who spoke French because they were from the southern part of Belgium. We had another four from the northern part of Belgium and they spoke Flemish. And we had four English speakers—a couple of Americans and two other guys who I think just spoke it because they couldn't communicate in French or Flemish. The three different groups kept to themselves and basically hated one another, and there wasn't anything I could do about it.

I did make some miscalculations. The biggest one was not really understanding that when I crossed over from England into continental Europe, it was a different style of basketball. Like I've said, basketball is basketball and 95 percent of it does translate across cultures and national boundaries. But you have to be aware of the 5 percent that doesn't.

In Belgium, the players did not enjoy the triangle offense and were resistant to it. They were used to structure—call the play, set the screen, go here, pass it there—and I was giving them more freedom than they wanted. The basketball in Belgium was higher quality but the game over in England was more Americanized.

I loved the triangle so much that I probably figured everybody would. I continued to run it, but I put in some other stuff—more of the orchestrated style they were used to.

Despite it all, the results were good. We were right there in the race for the regular season title, even though we had a zillion injuries and I ended up having to start guys on the second unit. They were eighteen, nineteen years old and they played their guts out. Some of them made their careers that season and went on to make a lot of money in Europe.

The team was owned by a big businessman in town, Rudolf Vanmoerkerke, whom everyone just called Mr. V. He had a travel company, owned an airline, and built the nice little arena that we played in—which was called Mister V-arena. It was a packed house every game. There wasn't much else in the way of sports other than a third- or fourth-division soccer club, so the fans and local press created a ton of pressure around us.

They wanted you to win every night and they wanted you to kill everybody—and they were critical of every single thing that happened. If you were up twenty points at the half and won the game by twenty-five, you'd actually get asked by one of the writers why you didn't win by forty. You know, like, *Did the team experience a letdown in the second half? Are you disappointed in that? We assume you'll address that at practice tomorrow morning, right?*

Basketball teams in Europe play in a number of in-season tournaments. We did well in the Euro Cup, making it to the final eight before getting beat by Rome, which was the best a Belgian team had done in about twenty years.

Normally, on Mondays, I'd get a call from one of the ladies in the team office, and she'd say, "Mr. V would like to meet you for lunch," and we'd go to his favorite restaurant and have sole and frites and talk about the weekend's game.

About two-thirds of the way through the season I got a call from a different woman I'd never heard from and she said, "You need to come to Mister V-arena." And she sounded nervous. She was like, "Come immediately. Hurry, hurry, hurry!"

It didn't seem like good news. I got there and was led into Mr. V's office.

Oostende was like the Israeli club Maccabi Tel Aviv—it was supposed to dominate its domestic rivals every season. Second place was an abject failure. We were doing well in the Belgian Cup, the in-season tournament, and were just one victory from being crowned champions. But I was not going to be around for that.

When I stepped into Mr. V's office, all he said was, "We have made a decision to change coaches," and he handed me a check for the rest of the season and that was that.

It didn't come as a complete shock. I'd had enough people putting mics in my face and saying, "Rumor has it if you don't win this weekend, you're out. Have you heard the same rumors? How do you feel about them?"

They'd come around the next Monday and say, "Well?" And I'd say, "I guess I've got to unpack again because it looks like I'm staying."

The timing of the firing did surprise me. We had won our game over the weekend—one of the young kids hit a shot at the buzzer for a one-point win—and had victories in something like eleven of our last thirteen games.

The timing was a little unfortunate in another way: my parents had flown in to visit with me. They had been at that last game and then I drove them to Paris, which was about three hours away. They were going to spend a couple of days there and then return and spend time in Oostende.

When they arrived back, I picked them up at the train station, told them what had happened, and said, "I don't really feel like hanging around here. Where should we go?" We decided on London and I loaded up my car, put it on the ferry, and we went over and saw a couple of shows and visited with my old college roommate, who had taken over for me as coach at Birmingham.

I'm sure I must have gone back after that to close up my apartment in Belgium and gather up whatever belongings I had there, but I have no memory of it.

At this point, you may be thinking, quite reasonably: Why didn't this man just come home? If he wanted to coach basketball, why did he not return to its worldwide capital, the good ole US of A, where the sport runs a little more logically and he probably wouldn't have to work for a Mr. V?

There are several answers. One is that in every job I was in, I felt like it was still possible for me to keep on learning and getting better. Even if no one else was taking notice, I believed I was becoming a really good basketball coach, and it looks now like I was right.

I was also, by and large, enjoying myself. In the years I was coaching overseas, during breaks in the basketball schedule, I spent time in the great cities of Europe—Paris, Amsterdam, Barcelona, and many others. My sister Maureen came over every year with her husband. We went to Greece, St. Moritz, Lake Como. In London, I went to the theater and the museums.

If things had gone differently when I was coaching college ball in the US, I suppose I could have moved on from South Dakota to a better assistant's job at a Division I school—and then on to another assistant's job—and then maybe a college head coaching job—or maybe skipped that and jumped over to the NBA to start moving up the pro coaching chain.

But I had a natural curiosity and maybe a wanderlust that goes back, at least in part, to my father telling me I wasn't leaving Iowa to go to Cornell. I'm not a better person than any other coach for the nontraditional path I took. But I'm pretty sure I'm a different person than I would have been.

When I coached the Canadian national team in the summer of 2019, we stopped in Australia to play some exhibition games on our way to the FIBA tournament in China. I took all the guys to the Sydney Opera House to see *West Side Story*. I know not all of them wanted to go, but I figured they'd thank me in twenty years. A few months before that, on an off night in New York, I arranged for our Raptors players to see *Hamilton* on Broadway.

It's not my job, of course, to show them this stuff, but I do feel it's a little bit of my responsibility. It's not going to hurt their basketball to open up their minds a little—and it might actually help.

There was one other reason—the biggest reason, to be honest—that I did not come back to the US sooner to coach. I couldn't make it happen.

I always returned in the summers. By that time, I'd be a little homesick. It wasn't terrible. But I did miss family and friends and some of the comforts of home, even the little silly stuff like Godfather's Pizza.

I'd hang out in Iowa and travel from there to basketball camps and wherever else I could make some contacts in the coaching fraternity. I definitely knew that I was going to have to resurface back in the States at some point.

The NBA Summer League takes place in Las Vegas now, and it's this big extravaganza. The gyms are sold out if a prized rookie is playing, and the games are all televised on ESPN. It's a way for the NBA to capture some attention in the dead of summer.

For many years, though, the Summer League took place in Long Beach, California, and it was more low-key—just a series of practices and games for teams to get a look at their draft picks and at other younger players who might have an outside chance of getting on a roster. But just like Las Vegas, it was a big gathering of people in the basketball universe—agents, scouts, team executives—and it functioned as a job fair for aspiring coaches.

The first summer I went was probably 1999. I was in between my two seasons of coaching the Manchester Giants, which is where I went after Belgium.

Long Beach is not one of the glamour spots on the Pacific Coast. It's a port and industrial town about twenty-five miles south of LA. I got a hotel for forty or fifty bucks a night and stayed for the month that the Summer League practices and games were taking place. I'd walk up the beach to the gym in the morning and back down the beach to my hotel at night.

I hung out that first summer trying to meet people. During conversations, I'd slip in every now and then that I was a coach and say something like, "If you know anybody who needs help on the sideline, I'm here the whole time. Just grab me."

There were plenty of other guys like me doing the same thing. I was networking or whatever you want to call it, but I had to force myself. I think it's fair to say that most of us Iowans are not natural networkers. I wasn't any good at it.

I came back to Long Beach the next year and I did better. I was given a team of free agents to coach. These were guys who went undrafted and could not get on the summer rosters of any of the NBA teams.

We did really well. We won some games and it was a pretty big thrill for me just to be on the sideline coaching in that setting. It wasn't like I was hanging out with Popovich, but he was there. Pat Riley was there.

From then on, I was working hard trying to get in the league. I was calling people, writing emails from England. But I didn't have the ideal profile. I wasn't connected to any famous coach. And I wasn't a former NBA player, and those were the guys they were trying to hire, which I totally understood. They had put their time in on the court and were getting a late start coaching.

David Kahn, the former president of the Minnesota Timberwolves, at one point owned four teams in the D-League and he had jobs open at all of them. I figured, that's a lot of open positions! I've got to have a shot at one of them, right? I reached out to him, but I never heard back.

In my heart, I wanted to be an NBA head coach. That was the dream. But I was not having conversations with people, even friends, and saying my goal is to coach in the NBA one day. It would have sounded stupid. The reality was that I couldn't even get an interview for a job as an assistant coach in the D-League.

⌃

Manchester, which I coached two seasons, from 1998 to 2000, was the most well-funded team in the British Basketball League.

Some fans considered it the evil empire, like the New York Yankees. They paid more than anybody else and had beautiful accommodations for the American players they brought over.

The owner was Bill Cook, a billionaire from Indiana who made his fortune in pharmaceuticals. The general manager, my boss, was Scott May, a former NBA player and one of the stars on Bobby Knight's undefeated 1976 national champions at Indiana.

The franchise was run very professionally and they were a notch above the rest of the league in every way but one: they almost never won anything. The first year I was with them we won the National Cup, one of the in-season tournaments. The second year we finished first ("top of the table") in the regular season, which is the big prize there.

After chasing a championship with a lot of money for years, they finally succeeded. That night, we were celebrating down in Wembley like you always do when you win a championship in England. And the owners gathered us together and took us across the street to a hotel lobby—the coaches, team executives and employees, a whole bunch of folks.

They gave us an extra $20,000 bonus and said, "We're selling the team. You're all free to go. It's over."

~

I would coach in England for another five seasons. All of it was useful. Looking back on it, none of it was exactly normal. (Did I reference Dennis Rodman a few chapters back? I'm getting there.)

To explain the full history and financial twists and turns of British professional basketball would take me hundreds of pages. But just to go through it really quickly, the league, depending on its sponsorship status, has been known by various names over the years. Just since 1990 it has been called the Carlsberg Basketball League, the Budweiser Basketball League, and the Dairylea Dunker's Championship. (If you don't know the name Dairylea, it's a popular brand of cheese over there.)

When I was still playing, I was awarded a case of Carlsberg beer when I got "man of the match." I gave it out in the locker room. No one that I'm aware of, under the Dairylea regime, ever got postgame cheese.

Unlike in the NBA and other US professional sports, which add new teams as the years go on and never subtract them—and where the rare struggling franchise picks up and moves to another city—British basketball teams often just go out of existence. The league made some bad decisions to become even more unstable—the main one being a shortsighted move to leave Sky TV and sign a contract for more money but with a less visible broadcast partner. In the US, it would be like leaving ESPN and jumping to a channel that reaches only half as many homes.

Several of the teams I coached are no longer around. The Birmingham Bullets, the longtime losing franchise where I won a championship in 1998, were liquidated in 2006. The Manchester Giants, the club that was so well funded that everyone resented them, hit the financial skids and went dark for a decade before resurfacing in 2012 under new ownership. There are two franchises in London at the moment, but neither is the London Towers—which is where I moved after the Manchester owners told us we were free to go and sent us away with our twenty grand.

The London job was like accelerated learning. Other British clubs had been invited before to play in the Euro League, which is the top level of basketball outside of the NBA, but usually did not have the money to make it work. The London Towers did.

There were some crazy stretches where we would play three nights in a row—Germany one night, Lithuania the next, and then back to London for the last one. I had a couple of different rosters. I would play certain guys in the Northern European League games (that was our section of the Euro League) and different ones when we competed against the teams in the British league.

We held our own most nights against the Euro competition and won our share of games, but we were up against some really top players. Pau Gasol, who would go on to win two NBA titles with the Lakers and make six NBA All-Star Games, was still playing for Barcelona. Back home, we won the regular season championship in the BBL.

The following season I joined the Brighton Bears as both the coach and part-owner. Very quickly after that, my partner made clear he had better things to do than run the team day-to-day.

Like a dumbass, I agreed to take on that role and also to become the sole owner. Keep in mind, this was not the same as assuming ownership of something with real value—it meant that I was the guy responsible for making payroll and keeping the lights on even if we were losing money. I also assumed the team's debts.

Brighton is a beautiful seaside town, an easy drive from London. Lots of people come for long weekends. Of all my stops, it was probably the most pleasant in terms of living in a cool place.

We played in two different arenas and the smaller one, downtown, held about 1,500 people. It was first come, first served—we had no real season ticket base—but before games there would be a line outside of people waiting along the beach. Tickets were really cheap, or some nights we would give a lot of them away. We were trying to get eyeballs, build interest.

We were also doing some incredible work in the schools—bringing in local kids and using our players to teach them basketball as well as reading and math skills. We hoped to attract more attention in the city and become a bigger presence, which might get us what we needed: more money in corporate sponsorships.

We had some on-court success, especially in the beginning, but it was a financial slog—and then, ultimately, a financial blood-bath. I spent a lot of time on non-basketball affairs: promoting the team, begging banks for lines of credit, trying to figure out, at one point, why our share of the league's TV money, which was supposed to fund our operations for the season, disappeared out of our accounts.

At the time I was coaching what would be my last season in Brighton, Dennis Rodman was on a London-based reality show called *Celebrity Big Brother*. It was one of those absurd but addictive shows, and it seemed like the whole country was watching it.

A friend of mine sent me an email suggesting I should try to get him to play for us when he got booted out of the house, and I said, "Yeah, that's a good idea," not really taking him seriously. But then he sent me an email contact for Rodman's manager. I got in touch with him and found out they were 100 percent interested. My first reaction was: Holy shit. But why not? Let's try to do this.

Then we found out the details. Rodman wanted $25,000 for each game he played, plus extras—his travel, hotel, lots of specifics about food and other stuff we should provide. To my shock, when I got in touch with the CEO of our main sponsor, he said, almost immediately, "I'm in," and agreed to put up the money.

The first game that Rodman played for us was at the 1,500-seat arena, which was attached to a community center and what was called a "multipurpose fun pool"—a splash pool with waterslides and so forth. So it wasn't exactly the United Center in Chicago.

Tickets sold out in a matter of hours. We put folding chairs in every space we could find, sold standing room, and probably stuffed five hundred more people into the gym. We issued about 175 media passes to journalists from all over Europe. This wasn't just unusual for British basketball—it was unprecedented.

The game was supposed to start at seven-thirty. At about seven-ten, Dennis still had not showed up. We got a call that he was late leaving London but should be at the arena soon. We pushed the game back to eight.

He got there at about seven-fifty—it took about eight security guards to get him out of his car and push him through the crowds gathered on the street—and he came into the locker room where everybody was sitting in their uniforms, waiting for him.

The first thing he said was, "Hey, I always shower before the game," and he dropped all his shit—his bag and whatever he was carrying—and walked into the shower room. When he came out and got his uniform on, we had a quick little meeting, just to let him know what we were running.

Everybody was nervous as hell, including me. I mean, yeah, he was in his mid-forties and he'd become this bizarre kind of celebrity—dated Madonna, in the tabloids all the time—but we were basketball people sitting in that locker room. To us, he was not a novelty act. He was Michael Jordan's former teammate on the Chicago Bulls championship teams. Phil Jackson's power forward. In his prime, he was one of the best damn players on the planet and he remains one of the greatest rebounders in the history of the sport.

As we were all together pregame, I began to tell him how we play, our offense and defense and so forth, and he stopped me and said, "I don't want to start. I want you guys to go do your thing and I'll come in off the bench."

A few minutes into the game, I put him in. I was still running the triangle, which of course he knew from Chicago, and one of the many options out of it is called the Blind Pig. You don't call the play; like everything else in the triangle, it's improvised.

The first offensive possession, Dennis flashed into the post. A guard passed him the ball and he immediately threw a no-look bounce pass to a cutting teammate for a basket. It was the Blind Pig, executed perfectly and instinctively, like he just made the same pass the day before with MJ on the receiving end.

He ran down to the defensive end, took a charge, and the building went absolutely crazy. He stretched out on the floor, and his new teammates, whom he'd met fifteen minutes ago, pulled him up off the floor and gave him high fives. We won the game by a few points and he scored a handful of points and grabbed maybe eight rebounds.

The second game he played was in the bigger arena. For some reason, I ended up riding with him to it in his limo. There was me, Dennis, his security guard, and Faria Alam—who was in the house with him on *Celebrity Big Brother*. She was one of these B stars whom everyone knew at the time because she was in the news for having an affair with the team manager of the national soccer team, which in England is a position of great prominence. She had been his secretary.

On the show, she and Dennis were trying to get together, but they couldn't in the house. It was an ongoing thing, a source of dramatic or sexual tension or whatever. But now they were out of the house. The show was over but there was still interest in them.

All these paparazzi were trailing us, and the next thing I knew, Faria was on the phone with her agent, who was screaming at her that she had to get out of the car. It's not a picture they wanted to see in the tabloids. She told the driver, "Pull over!" and jumped out.

We played the game and I went to a party afterward at a nightclub Dennis reserved. "Come on, Coach, you're going to the club," was how his invitation went.

Faria was there. Everyone was snapping her picture. I have no idea to this day why she had to jump out of the car—or why it was then okay to show up at the club.

Having had one game under his belt, Dennis had been more in the groove in the second game. He played thirty-eight minutes and pulled in twenty-three rebounds—which I thought was a damn good night for a forty-four-year-old guy who had been spending all his time on the set of a reality TV show.

There was all kinds of chaos afterward involving the league. (Of course there was.) They had wanted us to deactivate one of our American players for the games Rodman played—because he put us over the limit of our allowable non-English players— and I wouldn't do it. I figured this was their one chance to play alongside someone like Dennis and I wasn't picking a guy to miss it.

The coach of one of the teams we played complained, although he pretended to be nice about it. "It's wonderful people had the chance to see him play and it was a great experience for me and my players, but that isn't the point," he said. "It has been like a circus all week leading up to the game and now the BBL need to be seen to be strong in dealing with this."

We had to forfeit two wins, but I really didn't care. We had brought a ton of attention to British basketball, which it needed.

⌃

It's not an easy thing for me to look back on that last year in Brighton. The Rodman episode is funny, but it came about because we were in a really bad spot. (And Dennis, by the way, was a gentleman and a pleasure to coach. I saw him at the Las Vegas Summer League in 2019 and he gave me a big hug.)

One story in the British press, written after I won the title with the Raptors, said that it seemed I had "bitten off more than [I] could chew" in Brighton and it's hard for me to argue with that. I was spending probably 90 percent of my time on non-basketball stuff, trying to keep the thing afloat. I worked my ass off and there were a lot of sleepless nights. I drained my savings, such as they were.

At the end, as we were sinking financially, I was having a hard time paying the secretaries, ticket-takers, and other employees. Even so, I thought we were close to a significant new partnership, but the bank that held our line of credit was breathing down our neck. They wouldn't wait.

I went to the bank manager and was like, "Don't do it, man. You either wait six more months and you got a shot at getting your money back, or you get nothing."

He was a soccer guy. I think he was just tired of seeing Brighton Bears Basketball come across his desk.

The franchise folded when the season ended. As I've written, lots of basketball teams over there go belly-up. It's a normal occurrence, but when it happens, there has to be a villain, and it was me. I understood it. I was the owner, the responsible party.

I've mostly been able to distance myself. But when I won the title with the Raptors, I got lots of texts and emails letting me know that British basketball fans were following the games and rooting hard for us. They were proud and happy that someone who came out of the BBL was succeeding in the NBA. Hearing that was meaningful. It gave me hope that they would remember the good times and forget about how it ended.

5

AN IOWA HOMECOMING

HOW TO GET THE (BLEEP) BACK UP

Draft night with the Iowa Energy. *(Nurse family collection)*

There's a character in *Hamilton* named Hercules Mulligan who was a spy for the Continental Army, operating behind British lines. The show has very little profanity in it. But in one memorable lyric, in the song "Yorktown," Hercules proclaims: "When you knock me down, I get the fuck back up again."

That is not the worst motto for going forward in life. When I came home to Iowa in 2006, I had zero money. Literally zip. After a dozen years overseas, I had nine championships to my name, but nothing else.

A part of me sees this period of my life as such a downward spiral. I've never shared much of it because it feels embarrassing. But one of my big reasons for doing this book is a feeling that I may have some inspiration to put out into the world—some lessons on how to get back up after you've been knocked on your ass. That's a big part of sports. A big part of trying to achieve any kind of success or happiness.

Just a dozen years after leaving Brighton, I became head coach of an NBA team. Even now, that seems a little unlikely. There was some luck and good timing involved. But much more so, there was an intensity of work and self-belief on my part.

⌃

I moved in with my sister and her family in Des Moines when I returned and was working as a fitness trainer and private basketball coach. One afternoon I was driving on I-235, which goes right through the heart of Des Moines, and I passed by the new Wells Fargo Arena. It was about a year old and hard to miss since part of it hangs over the highway. I knew the area because it was right next to Veterans Memorial Auditorium, where my high school team won the state title.

I pulled off at an exit, got the number for the arena, and called in and asked for the general manager. I wasn't famous at that point (nor am I really now) but I was maybe a little bit Iowa famous. The guy on the other end of the phone thought he recognized my name. "Aren't you the guy who played at Northern Iowa?" he asked me.

That established that I was not just some random nut calling in from the side of the road. I told him a little bit about what I had been up to in recent years and then said, "This is a beautiful-looking arena. You guys really ought to have a D-League team in here."

He agreed. "We'd love that," he said, which was all I needed to set off on a quest.

I did a ton of research on the size of the markets of the D-League teams at the time. Many of them were a whole lot smaller than Des Moines, which has more than two hundred thousand residents and is almost twice as big as any other city in the state. The D-League was playing in places like Erie, Pennsylvania; Canton, Ohio; and Portland, Maine—way smaller cities than Des Moines.

I made contact with people at the NBA offices in New York and then with D-League executives in Charlotte. I put together numbers on the size of the Des Moines market and the projected fan base and revenue and possible sponsors.

I had, of course, been involved in all of this stuff in Brighton. I knew the language. But now I was in a city and a state that

I knew, from my own experience, absolutely loved basketball. If we did it right, they would embrace it.

I wasn't looking to own a team. God no, not after what I'd just been through. I wanted to get someone else interested in that. But in my mind, I was going to coach a team if we could get one. I had not succeeded in breaking into the pro ranks in the US in any other way, so why not create a damn team I could coach?

Iowa is crazy for minor-league baseball. There are teams in Des Moines, Cedar Rapids, Quad Cities, Burlington, Clinton, Sioux City, Waterloo, and Clarinda.

Various minor-league basketball teams over the years had failed. None of them, though, were in anything as organized or as well funded as the D-League, which had direct NBA backing (like baseball's minor leagues are backed by big-league clubs)— and none played in an arena like the new Wells Fargo.

I made my way to the man in town everyone said I had to talk to—Jerry Crawford, a big lawyer and a political and civic activist. He dabbled in various sports, including owning some racehorses.

The first time we talked was on the phone. As I got partway into my pitch, he stopped me, and I'll never forget what he said. His exact quote was: "Not another fucking minor-league basketball team, right?"

Over time, I wore Jerry down. He brought in other partners and they set about trying to get a team. On February 7, 2007, the D-League named four new franchises and one of them was Des Moines. I was named the coach of this team, just as I had hoped.

I got involved in all the organizational stuff, including what the team was going to be called. We had a contest and a lot of names were suggested, most of them not good. The Corncobs and the Scarecrows were two that surfaced. We settled on the Iowa Energy. (As an affiliate of the Minnesota Timberwolves, in the G League, they are now called the Iowa Wolves.)

We were not going to have our first game for about another nine months and I needed something to do and an income. One day I went to this huge AAU tournament. In the decade I had been gone, I heard a lot about AAU ball, and I wanted to see what it was all about.

The tournament was in the town of Ankeny, a Des Moines suburb. As soon as I walked in, I could see how the youth basketball scene had blown up. The bleachers were packed with parents—there were dozens of teams all around—and there were people in the hallways. You could hardly move.

When I started watching the games, the other thing I noticed was that the quality of play was bad, especially the shooting. The ball did not go in the hoop at any reasonable kind of percentage because nobody shot it with proper form—meaning footwork, angle of the wrist and elbow, backspin on the ball.

Shooting had been my thing for as long as I'd been involved in basketball and it was always going to be a way for me to make a few bucks if all else failed. I decided I would run shooting camps.

I went back to my place and wrote out a letter. It said, basically: *My name's Nick Nurse. I come from a small Iowa town and I played Division I basketball, and the only reason I could play is because I could shoot the ball. I went to Europe for ten years to coach and now I'd like to teach your kid to become a better shooter.*

There's a fine line between entrepreneurial and desperate. I'm not sure which side I was on. I started going to more tournaments and handing the letter out to people in the stands. I put it on car windshields in the parking lots.

I had gone to a seminar on internet marketing, which was a newer thing at the time. I pumped out material every day and figured out where to target it. I pretty quickly built up a nice little business and was running shooting camps all over the area. I taught the fundamentals that many players, even really good ones, either ignore or never knew.

I have never not been a shooting coach. In Toronto, I teach my players how to do it—and my assistant coaches how to teach it. Few things irritate me more than when I see a coach just rebounding the ball and throwing it back to players without looking closely at form and correcting it. I sometimes say: if we just wanted a rebounder, I could hire a high school kid.*

Since we're on the subject—and for those of you who would like to go out to the driveway or gym to put these into practice— here, briefly, are the basics of what I taught to the kids who signed up for my camp, and what I teach to this day in the NBA.

- Line up your shooting foot—the right foot for right-handers— directly with the center of the rim. Make sure to keep your feet spread far enough apart that you have proper balance.
- Keep the fingers and thumb on your shooting hand relaxed. You cannot shoot well if you're squeezing the ball.
- Your index finger and middle finger should go around the center stripe of the ball, or around the air hole. This is super important because that's the middle of the ball.

---

* In our championship season, the Raptors were fourth in the league in "true shooting percentage," which is a combination of two-point shots, three-pointers, and free throws. Our rankings, as we both taught better shooting form and strategized ways to get better shots, had been steadily rising year to year.

- Your other hand guides the ball as you raise it to shoot—but it is uninvolved as you let the ball go. Releasing the shot is a one-handed process and has been since the two-handed set shot went out of fashion about seventy years ago.

- Bring the ball straight up with your wrist cocked and release with your elbow locked and arm extended straight at the target. The ball should roll off the middle and index fingers, giving it perfect symmetrical spin. I call this the "flight spin," and not the more commonly used "backspin," because doing it correctly not only makes the ball land more softly if it hits the rim, but also makes it fly straight. If you release a shot with side spin, it may subtly curve like a baseball pitcher's breaking ball.

There was one other important aspect of my instruction: I designed a basketball that served as a teaching aid. It was red, white, and blue, and we put a stripe down the middle, with painter's tape, so a shooter would know exactly where to grip it. At my camps, we had lines on the floor pointing toward the hoops, and shooters could use those lines and the marking on the center of the ball as they set up to shoot. It amounted to quick visual teaching on how to release the ball straight with backspin.

I ordered really good balls, in bulk, from a company in New York and had them doctored up at a family reunion. We basically had an assembly line going.

You may have heard a basketball referred to as "the pill" if you've ever played pickup on the playground. If you take a shot instead of passing to an open teammate, you're likely to hear someone yell, "Pass the damn pill!"

I named my special basketball in honor of this playground slang. It was called the Nurse's Pill. We had a company mass-produce them (no more painter's tape).

The basketball has lettering that says, THE NURSE'S PILL, and under that is the slogan: "Your Prescription to Better Shooting." I have to say, it's a sharp-looking item. (And still available on eBay and in other corners of the internet!)

⌃

The Iowa Energy played its first game on November 23, 2007. We defeated the Dakota Wizards, the league's defending champion.

Three nights later we took the floor at the Wells Fargo for the first time and it was a sensational evening. We came out in our eye-catching uniforms—purple, orange, and red—and won again, defeating the Albuquerque Thunderbirds. The attendance of 8,842 set a new D-League record.

The victories were by a combined five points, the beginning of a season-long pattern: the games in the D-League tended to be really close, and we didn't win enough of them. We would finish the season with a record of 22-28, missing the playoffs.

The "D" in the D-League stood, of course, for "developmental," meaning, primarily, the development of players—but every coach wants to win. It is part of our competitive nature. And just like the players, we were in a developmental phase, fighting for our careers. I needed to keep the job I had (I was not going back to England a third time) and put myself in a position to get a better one.

One big challenge of the D-League is that players come and go quickly. You lose your best guys when they get called up to the NBA, replace them, and then quite often they end up back with you after they're cut loose. The back end of your roster is constantly in flux because you're trying guys out.

When our first season ended, I sat down with my staff and said: How can we design offensive and defensive systems, as well as terminology, that can be learned really quickly? How can we refine our system to what they can handle?

I don't want my teams to necessarily play with less complexity than our opponents. The system has to have some variance to it—a range of ways to attack and defend. But what I wanted to do after that first season in Iowa was figure out how to *teach* the way we play with less complexity.

We spent a good bit of time just thinking up what we were going to call our different offensive plays and defensive coverages—numbers or colors or other words that players could easily remember. We established the principles we would hammer into players. On defense, for example, the principles were *pressure the ball, contest shots,* and *block out on rebounds.* Every single thing we did was built out from that foundation and it enabled players to more easily grasp the finer details.

What I learned in the NBA is that this kind of teaching— concise, easily understood, putting bedrock principles before the granular detail—is no less important. And for many of the same reasons as in the D-League—including the fact that you can come in to work one day and be looking at several new faces.

The NBA trade deadline comes after we've played about two-thirds of the schedule, just as we are entering the home stretch leading into the playoffs. A crazy number of players change teams at the deadline, sometimes more than 10 percent of the league, and it's not unusual for teams—even good ones contending for the NBA title—to end up with new players in the starting lineup. No other pro sport experiences such roster chaos so late in the season.

And keep in mind that on a basketball team, switching out just one starter constitutes a 20 percent change in the starting lineup. Between starters and subs, most teams play an eight- or nine-man rotation, so switching out two or three of them, which isn't uncommon, amounts to massive change.

The D-League was great preparation for the NBA's roster upheavals because down there it happened all the time. You had a group of guys—they came together, developed roles—and then they'd all leave, and you had to do it again.

And this would happen like ten times. One day you had team chemistry and the next you were coaching a group of strangers.

I've written about an intensity of effort, and by that, I mean an utter and complete devotion to getting better at your chosen field. It's only basketball in my case. I believe it has value—the product we put on the floor entertains people, and sometimes serves as a needed diversion in difficult times—but I know its relative importance. There's a long list of people doing more vital work—doctors, nurses, teachers, scientists, mail carriers, social workers, farmers. Hell, carpenters and plumbers, too.

But the lessons that can be drawn from how I have approached my work and career are universal: you get out of it what you put in.

In the D-League, any night we weren't playing, I watched NBA games on TV with a whiteboard on my lap. During time-outs, I would draw a play for the team with the ball. What would get them a basket? Would my play match what the NBA coach drew up?

I did the same thing when I was in England, viewing the

games on those VHS tapes that got routed through Germany. The plays had already been run, days before, but it didn't matter. I was rehearsing for when I got my shot.

I'm sure that seems a little crazy or obsessive but it helped me. I tell young coaches they ought to do the same thing—don't just watch a game from your couch; put yourself in the mind of the head coach. I don't know how many take me up on it.

In an NBA game, you've got about twenty seconds to draw up a play at a time-out and then you have to communicate it to your team. The music in the arena is blasting at like a zillion decibels. It's not that easy. If you see a team come out of a stoppage in play and look like they didn't all run the same play, or they don't run a play that looked like something a coach would have wanted, there's a reason for it: it probably did not get drawn up or communicated effectively enough for everyone to be on the same page.

If you could have looked in on me the summer after my first season in Iowa, it might have been a little alarming. I lived in a pretty nice place adjoining a golf course, but I didn't play very often and I'm not sure how much I even got outside. Probably mostly just for meals.

I was pissed that we didn't do better, and what hit me really hard was how close the games were. It seemed like every one that we lost came down to the last couple of possessions. If I designed better plays at the end, if we did a better job executing them, or if our players understood better what I wanted, we easily could have turned half a dozen games around and made the playoffs.

As a coach, when you don't win, you can complain about your players' efforts. You can whine that you weren't provided better players. Or, you can look inward and examine what you could have done to put them in better positions to succeed.

My assistant coach was Nate Bjorkgren, whom I later hired for my staff in Toronto. He played for me at South Dakota and then became a high school coach. He was as hungry as I was.

In Iowa that first season, he worked as a volunteer before we were able to give him a paid position the next year. He often paid for his own flights to away games, or if a game was within a couple hundred miles, he drove. I'd pay for his meals.

Nate and I spent the months after the season in my basement, holed up like survivalists. I put up dry-erase boards on every wall. Day in and day out, we plotted how we could improve offensively, how we could get better defensively, what we could do differently in terms of player personnel. Once we came up with something, it would go on a spreadsheet, so we would be running back and forth between the whiteboards and the computer.

That first year had been like a testing ground. The day it ended, we went after it, all summer long, to get ready for the second year. It had taken me a long time to break in to coaching at the professional level in the US, and I didn't want it to end abruptly.

Because of all the close games we lost, we spent a lot of those hours imagining every possible end-of-game scenario we could think of and drawing up schemes to win games.

We would be like, "Okay, we're down two points, six seconds to go, and inbounding underneath the other team's basket. Let's draw up a play. Now let's do it from half-court. Still six seconds left, but we're down three so we need a three-point shot."

We'd keep changing it up: "We're under the hoop and the score is tied, but now we only have a second and a half. We're on the left sideline. Now, the right."

We'd have notations all over the board. *Put our offensive subs in ASAP. Do we have a time-out left? Can we run the baseline? Is the other team over the foul limit? Are we?*

Every one of these answers led to a different scenario, a different play call. We'd draw something up and I'd say, "This ain't right, Nate," and we'd erase it and go with something else.

Then we would reverse it—the other team had the ball and we're on defense. Pick them up full court? Guard the inbounds pass or double-team their best ball handler to keep it out of his hands? If we're up three points, do we foul them and put them on the line? With how many seconds left? Do you do one thing on the road and another at home?

People would say, how can you spend all that time in there? How many variables are there? Well, the variables are infinite. As many as you want to run.

At the end of the summer, every single whiteboard, all around the basement, was filled. They had been filled multiple times. We took pictures and then erased the boards to make more room.

I came up with a philosophy that would guide us going forward: every time we practice, we're going to put up on the scoreboard that the score is tied, 90–90, and there are three minutes left. Or sometimes we'll make it just one minute left.

I do the same thing now with the Raptors. Tons of end-of-game situations at practices. It focuses the mind. There are no harmless turnovers when you practice like that, no casually missed shots. It all counts.

After we focused our practices in Iowa on how we would win at the end of games—after that summer Nate and I spent in the basement—we turned it around. Over the next three seasons, our record was a combined 102-48.

It was a big learning point for me. I know that the D-League back then, and the G League now, is off the radar for most fans. But these were the highest-quality players I had ever coached, and after a year of not exactly figuring it out, I felt like I had learned how to make them win.

We won the D-League championship in 2011. There was another little victory wrapped up in that championship: in one of the playoff games at Wells Fargo Arena, we drew 14,036 fans—another record for the D-League and confirmation that Des Moines, despite predictions to the contrary, was ready for "another fucking minor league basketball team."

^

I was tested by the difficult road I took as well as enriched by it.

Even the most junior assistant at a high Division I program in NCAA basketball makes a good salary. He flies charter and stays at good hotels. The same is true for young NBA assistants, except that the hotels are better—instead of the Marriott, they stay at the Ritz or Four Seasons.

I didn't have any of that for a long time. Not in England or the D-League. It gave me a certain mindset. It made me recognize a kind of hunger in some players, and how, as a coach, I could tap into that.

I've told the story of Nate and me to young coaches. It's funny. It's entertaining. Everybody gets a kick out of it. Two guys in a basement, pizza boxes strewn all over, imagining game scenarios while scribbling all over whiteboards.

It's the hoops version of that movie *A Beautiful Mind*. But instead of brilliant mathematical equations, we're drawing up sideline out-of-bounds plays.

But here's the thing. When I talk about how we made a

spreadsheet of all the stuff we put on the dry-erase boards, I get asked by young coaches: Can we have that? They want the work product without doing the work.

And I say, no, you're missing the whole damn point. You have to do it yourself.

^

FREEDOM IN THE HUDDLE

LESSONS FROM DR. VICTORY

The 1985 Kuemper Catholic state championship team.

(Courtesy of Kuemper Catholic School System/Niceswanger Photography)

On the day I was named coach of the Toronto Raptors, I called Darrell Mudra, who is one of the greatest coaches almost no one has ever heard of.

He was eighty-nine at the time and living quietly in retirement at his home in the Florida Panhandle. The press conference announcing my hiring was about to take place. His wife always answered the phone, and when she handed it to him, I said, "Hey, man, I'm getting ready to be named the coach of the Toronto Raptors. I just wanted you to know before you saw it on TV."

The title of this chapter is a tribute to Mudra and his book— *Freedom in the Huddle: The Creative Edge in Coaching Psychology.* I first came across it more than three decades ago, and there is virtually nothing that I do now that cannot be traced back, in some way, to its author and his philosophies.

Many years later, after I finally got to meet Phil Jackson, I sent him Mudra's book as a gift. It was out of print and hard to find (I still had my own treasured copy), so I paid something like $85 for it.

Mudra's interest was not in the technical aspects of sports or how to draw up great plays—the Xs and Os, to use that term. All that game strategy is important, but a great coaching career is rarely built on those things because if you come up with anything truly innovative, it will quickly be stolen.

His great insights were in the realm of leadership: how to motivate players and how to get individuals with disparate personalities and priorities to come together as one cohesive unit.

Mudra played fullback at Peru State in Nebraska and from there set off on a long coaching odyssey. (Which, as you might imagine, I can relate to.) He started off coaching both basketball and football at a couple of different small-town high schools in Nebraska. He moved on to become an assistant college football coach at three colleges—and then the head football coach at Adams State, North Dakota State, Arizona, Western Illinois, Florida State, Eastern Illinois, and then, finally, Northern Iowa.

He won just about everywhere he went, earning him the nickname Dr. Victory. (He had a doctorate in education.) His specialty was taking over losing teams and turning them around instantly.

His first team, at Adams State in Colorado, had been 1-8 the previous year; in Mudra's initial season, they went 8-1. At Eastern Illinois, his team went 12-2 a year after it had finished 1-10 under the previous coach.

He took a little longer to turn things around at Arizona, which had won a total of six games in the two previous seasons before he arrived in 1967. That first year he had a rare losing season, but in the second one Arizona finished 8-3 and went to the Sun Bowl—back when it was a lot harder to get in a bowl game.

Mudra was decades ahead of his time in his thinking, and some of his unorthodox methods still have not caught on. The most obvious of those is that on game days he coached from the press box and communicated to his sideline over a headset—and even then, only sparingly. He figured he had done his work during the week, and after that, the game belonged to the players.

I first became aware of Mudra in the mid-1980s when I was at Northern Iowa, his last coaching stop. He was fit-looking with a flowing head of black hair. One Saturday afternoon when I was in the stands, a few minutes before the kickoff of a home game, I saw him sprint through the crowd and up into the press box, which I thought was pretty cool.

Around that time, my brother Steve gave me his book. I'm sure I looked at it, but I didn't give it a lot of thought; I was still thinking I was going to be an accountant. I didn't engage with it until several years later, when I became an assistant at South Dakota and began to understand that coaching is a subject that demands a lifetime of study.

I wrote Mudra a letter back then, telling him that I was trying to use some of his methods. It was the beginning of a long dialogue, one that's been ongoing for more than a quarter century.

⌃

Mudra wrote: "Leadership must be defined in such a way that true leaders can be distinguished from mere power holders."

That may not seem like a revolutionary thought now—certainly not in modern workplaces where there has been a de-emphasis on top-down management and lots of talk about empowering employees. (How much of that is just talk as opposed to reality, I can't say.) But it was an outside-the-box idea when Mudra started coaching in the early 1950s, and even when he published his book in 1986. In those days, the model of a coach was still a Vince Lombardi type, an almighty power high above the group.

Mudra's philosophies still cut across the grain of traditional notions of leadership. He writes that the "authoritarian principle" holds that "a team cannot be run by several people at the same time." He preferred a "democratic principle," with the head coach as "merely an executor for the group."

That last thought explains why Mudra felt comfortable hiking upstairs and watching games from the press box. It was his signal to the assistant coaches, and even more so, his players, that they were empowered. Victory or defeat was in their hands.

Mudra's principles involve a head coach surrendering a great deal of power. It's not easy to do and I'm not sure I could follow them all even if I wanted to. He coached primarily in smaller college settings, in "learning environments," to use that term. The NBA is a whole different deal.

The thirty franchises are worth an average of nearly $2 billion each. The head coach is a team's most visible management employee, and owners do expect us to run things with a pretty firm hand. While it might be fun and sort of interesting for me to run up to the press box one game and coach from there, I'm not real sure how it would go over.

But many of Mudra's broader principles are more realistic to put into practice. One is: ask your players questions and listen closely to their answers. You don't do this as an exercise to make them feel included—you do so out of a conviction that what they tell you is going to help you win games.

My time in Birmingham is a good example of this. Looking back on it, I'm sure I still seemed like a kid to some of my players. I was twenty-seven years old. I had been gone from England for four years before returning for a second tour and I didn't know what was going on in the league.

Tony Dorsey and Nigel Lloyd were my best players, veteran guys—Nigel's ten years older than I am—and I asked them, how do you want to run this offense? Do you want the ball on this block or that block? Left side or right side?

After I heard what they said, I'd respond, Okay, we'll get everything set up so you get the ball where you need it. It made sense to me. It was not about giving up my power to the players—it was about tapping into their knowledge.

This was the same team that told me before a championship game they didn't want to play the junk defense we had put on the London Towers earlier in the year. They wanted to guard them straight up. It didn't occur to me to push back then—and it doesn't now when my players speak up. I don't always agree but I'm never going to be a brick wall.

It's possible that I am more open to hearing my players because I started coaching so young. It would have been stupid (and probably disastrous) for me to act like they did not possess some wisdom that I lacked. I got used to listening.

And my playing experience probably made me more inclined toward it—my high school football coach letting me call my own plays, my basketball coaches in both high school and college allowing me to lead the team on the floor. It wasn't the norm back then, and in football it still isn't.

The higher the stakes are, the less likely it is that a coach will cede some control. NFL quarterbacks get plays called into their headsets and can communicate with coaches until fifteen seconds before the ball must be snapped. They don't allow that in college, so you see the quarterbacks peering at all those crazy signs being flashed on the sideline.

I understood even back in high school and college that what my coaches were doing was a little unusual. I don't remember *asking* to call my own plays. But I did feel strongly that I could see and feel things that they couldn't because I was on the court or playing field—and that in crucial moments, I may have a better idea of what would work.

As an NBA head coach, I hold the whiteboard at time-outs, and I call plays at crucial moments. I have the last word. But if my point guard or other smart, veteran players tell me what they want to run, I hear them out.

Other aspects of Mudra's guidance are not as easily grasped because they really challenge coaching orthodoxy. For example: Do not expect your players to be selfless. Do not even expect them to always put team and winning first. Every player, Mudra wrote, "has goals that are more important than winning, and they have many loyalties."

That sounds like everything your eighth-grade basketball coach tried to beat out of you. The myth was you always gave yourself fully to the team. One hundred percent. If you scored two points or thirty—or even if you rode the bench the entire game—it didn't matter as long as the team won. You were happy and content.

What I learned from Mudra, and what I know from my years of coaching, is that a big part of my job is to recognize my players' selfish goals—in all their particulars—and then find a way to make them come into line with the team's need to win.

It's another thing that I started doing in England. When I was coaching Tony Dorsey, I would leave him in the game at times even when we were comfortably ahead. The first time I did he sort of looked at me, and I said, "Listen, you need to score a couple of quick baskets to get to thirty points, because we're going to get you the MVP in this league."

I knew he wanted that and knew it would increase his value in the marketplace. It made sense for me on various levels to help him achieve that. (Tony won the MVP on two different teams that I coached in England.)

In the NBA, I have players who have just signed huge, multi-year contracts and want to prove they're worth the money they've just been given. They feel they should score a certain number of points a game and get a certain number of rebounds or assists.

Do I sometimes leave one of them in longer than I might otherwise in a game that's out of reach in order for them to meet those goals? Yes. It is not in my interest, or my team's, for a star to feel like less than a star. At crunch time in an NBA game, we depend on alphas playing like alphas. I'm not here to bring them down to earth.

I have other players in the last year of their contracts who are playing for their next contract. And I have players at the end of the bench whose deepest need is to stay on the roster and build a career. None of these are team goals, exactly—but if handled correctly by the players and the coach, they should all help the team.

Think about this last category of player for a moment, the one struggling for a foothold in the league, and consider how the NBA is structured. There are thirty teams and each of them has fifteen players on its active roster—meaning there are 450 full-fledged players in the league. That is a tiny number considering how many players are competing to get into the NBA from across the country and around the world. (It is also a small number compared to the number of slots on pro football and baseball rosters—or the couple thousand roster spots available in the top soccer leagues in England, Italy, Spain, and Germany.)

Now imagine all the pipelines leading into the NBA. There are about 4,500 kids on Division I college basketball scholarships at any given time, and a whole lot of them believe (however incorrectly) that they have some legitimate shot at the NBA. There are some three hundred players on D-League rosters, many of them former top college players and every one of them gunning to get into the league. Several hundred more players are competing in good professional leagues in Europe, Asia, and Australia.

What is the difference in talent level between the bottom 150 players in the NBA—the subs who usually only play in the event of injuries or when a game is a blowout—and the next best 150 who are knocking on the door? It's not a lot.

Show me two of these players head-to-head and I'll definitely have a preference and a reason for keeping one over the other. But some other coach may have a different opinion. Lots of times, players are elevated into the league just because they got the right opportunity with the right team at the right time.

A roster spot is just a first step. After that, younger guys must then break into the regular playing rotation—usually consisting of just eight to ten players—to establish themselves. The ones who succeed can set themselves up for long careers and tens of millions of dollars in salary. The result of a young player getting a shot is often a veteran losing his place in the rotation and suddenly looking at what could be the beginning of the end of his career.

In either case—for the younger players or the older ones—it's a heavy burden for them. As a coach, I deal with it head-on. (Remember the bronze elephant on my desk—the elephant in the room?) I address their personal goals and I do it directly.

To give one example, I've had to have talks with a couple of Raptors players, former high draft picks, still in their mid-twenties, who had already been traded a couple of times and had just landed on our roster. With one of them in particular, his star was fading, and quickly. I told him, look, you're inefficient. You take too many difficult shots, commit too many turnovers, and don't produce enough good stuff on the other side of the ledger. You can't help us if you keep playing like that.

I told him exactly what he had to do to get on the court: play with energy, take better shots, move the ball quickly rather than stopping it with individual play.

I was just as direct about what he would get in return: If you do the shit we want you to do, I'll put you in a position to thrive. If you don't, you're not going to play, and I don't know what's going to happen to your career after that.

Think of it as a package I'm putting together for you, I said. In every game, you should be able to get three free throws, take a couple of three-pointers, get one or two put-back baskets, and I'll give you a couple of isolation opportunities. You'll end up with eleven, twelve, maybe thirteen points off the bench. And you'll do it at an efficient rate, and you'll have value in the marketplace.

That was not exactly "putting the team first"—but if this guy could do all that, he surely was going to help us.

The D-League taught me to help players manage their aspirations and fears. Very few of them had a team-first mindset and I did not expect them to. As Mudra wrote, they had "many loyalties" and their first was to their own careers.

On a human level, it was hard for a lot of them. They held on to hope—that's what the league is all about—while knowing they could be one step away from career death.

The experience was nothing that they ever imagined. Many were stars on the AAU circuit, teenagers who not that long before were sorting through piles of mail from famous college coaches—fielding their phone calls—and deciding which schools to visit and which ones to cross off their lists. That's a heady thing. Their decision process gets followed closely by recruiting "gurus" and put on social media. It's hard for any of those kids not to get inflated opinions of themselves and not to project forward to an NBA career and the lifestyle that comes with it.

The D-League is packed with guys like this. Many played for top D-I programs—the blue bloods like Duke, Kentucky, Kansas, and UNC and on down the list. They dressed and trained in facilities that were equal to, or in some cases better than, those afforded to NBA players.

Some of them stayed in college for just a year or two before deciding to turn pro, and that's when reality hit. The control they felt as top prospects was suddenly gone. Some found out they were not good enough to get drafted or catch on in the league as free agents. Others made it into the league briefly before getting bounced out, and now they're in the D-League fighting for a second chance and trying to deal with the strain of it all as well as a day-to-day existence that was not something they ever anticipated.

When I coached the Iowa Energy, the league rule was that teams did not take a plane if the trip was ten hours or less—so we bused to Fort Wayne and Sioux Falls. On the longer trips, we usually got to the airport at something like five-thirty in the morning and connected through Detroit or Minneapolis. The big guys would be begging for exit rows because we'd take multiple flights, often on cramped commuter planes.

Players who had only performed in front of packed houses in Chapel Hill found themselves playing in front of nobody in Fort Wayne. And the hardest part was that the basketball itself, the competition on the floor, was way better than they ever faced.

A star on a top NCAA team plays most of his games against lesser competition. Hell, two-thirds of the teams on their schedules have no chance of beating them. Their practices include non-scholarship walk-ons, kids who might be a foot shorter and can't guard them.

In the D-League, they are up against grown men every night.

A young guy just a year out of one of those blue-blood schools might find himself matched up against a player in his mid-twenties from a "lesser" program. The other guy is six years older—he's stronger and smarter—and he's just as desperate.

Plus, he's got a chip on his shoulder because you're from Duke and he played at Austin Peay. He's going to kick your ass and enjoy the hell out of it.

That's the D-League in a nutshell. Survival of the fittest. I like to think that anyone who comes out of there emerges as a better person, and probably a more grateful one. That goes for coaches as well as players.

⌃

At the beginning of the D-League seasons, I'd have a meeting with my team and say we have two goals: one of them is to win and the other is to get a whole bunch of you into a better situation.

For some, that meant the NBA, but I also talked a lot about Europe. I'd tell them: just do what you need to do to stay on this roster. We only have eight or ten guys at a given time. You're going to get your chances. If you average sixteen points a game and fill up some of the other box score lines—rebounds, assists, steals—someone will want you. It was like a mantra: Stick with it. Get better. And something good will happen for you.

The D-League minimum salary back then was just $15,000 for the six-month season. (In the G League now, it is $35,000.)

Some of my players had kids. They had wives or girlfriends. In Europe, there was the potential to make six figures. Hundreds of American players have built long careers over there. It's not the NBA, but it can be a really good life.

I think some of my D-League players were a little disoriented. They were one step away from the NBA but just a short drop from not playing basketball anymore.

When I think about the problems our society faces, I'd rank entitlement as pretty high up on the list. Somewhere after mass shootings, the rising cost of education, and maybe a couple of other things. My players had lost the sense of entitlement they once had. They'd been knocked down a few notches. Some of them played with a sense of desperation. I didn't have to get them to try harder—I had to calm them down.

We worked hard at building up their individual skills. I was just about a one-man show at the beginning in Iowa: coach, general manager, player development coordinator, and a whole lot else.

On off nights, or late at night after we had played, I'd watch NBA games on television and also D-League games, which were streamed on the internet, in order to see what kinds of trades we could make.

I was living on the phone, mostly talking to agents, who would call and bitch at me. *My guy doesn't have enough minutes. He's playing the wrong position. He doesn't get enough shots. What the hell is going on?* They'd go on and on to the point that sometimes I'd do one of those things where you hold the phone away from your ear and wait for them to stop.

The agents were hustling just like the players were. (And like I was.) Some of them didn't have any clients yet in the NBA, or maybe just a few. If they got one of my guys in the league, that could lead them to signing more clients, and probably better ones.

In the beginning, they didn't know me. Nobody did. I was the new guy from the British Basketball League. I think half of them were surprised when I didn't talk with an English accent.

But I started getting players called up to the NBA, and all of a sudden it changed. It went from *who the hell are you?* to *let's get my player on Nurse's team because it gives him the best chance of moving up.*

I would get calls from an NBA general manager who was hit with injuries and he'd ask me who the best player on my team was. I'd tell him whom he should take, and boom, that guy would be gone. I never hesitated because we needed to win a game or because we had our own injuries. I do think some other D-League teams did do that, but my first priority was to get guys promoted.

In my four years in Iowa, we had sixteen call-ups. It was crazy. I think the next-closest team had three. If you add in my two years with the Rio Grande Valley Vipers, twenty-three of my players went up to the NBA. It's different now with the G League, where teams function almost like Triple-A affiliates of Major League Baseball teams and there's a lot of back-and-forth movement.[*]

The guys we sent up to the NBA from the D-League did not always even get to play, and as soon as the big team got healthy, they came back to us. They were in that really tenuous spot I described—that big pool of players from around the world vying for the last couple of seats on an NBA bench.

But if they made it up even just on a ten-day contract, they earned some money—probably as much as their whole D-League season was going to pay. And they had a pedigree for life: they had been in the NBA, and that could help them get a job in Europe.

---

[*] On our 2019–20 Raptors team, I might have as many as four guys who spend time with our G League team, Raptors 905, which plays in the Toronto suburb of Mississauga.

And we did have several who latched on and stayed. One of my players from the 2007–08 Iowa Energy, Anthony Tolliver, went from us to a brief stay with a club in Germany and is now in his twelfth NBA season. He's played for nine different teams and while he has never been a star, he is a solid contributor and has made himself many millions of dollars.

And, by the way, helping push a player forward pays dividends beyond just that one guy. Anthony has paid some of his good fortune forward and is among a group of NBA players who founded an organization to dig new wells to provide clean water in East Africa.

If you're a basketball coach who believes in Mudra's concepts— surrendering some control, trusting the decision-making of the athletes on the floor, unleashing their creativity—it helps to have a good point guard whom you can trust and communicate with.

It's not like I learned that for the first time in the D-League, but it was really driven home by my experience with Curtis Stinson, who played the position for me in Iowa and was the leader I needed.

Most coaches would say that point guards are the extensions of ourselves on the court. They have the ball in their hands more than any other player, even in an era of what is being called positionless basketball. They call out the plays and they convey messages back and forth between the bench and the other four players on the floor.

When the action gets fast and furious, they calm things down. They're the last line of defense against chaos, which in the D-League was crucial with so many guys coming and going.

I've been fortunate to have really cool relationships with point guards, but Curtis was, in a way, the prototype. He grew up in the Bronx and played collegiately for Iowa State. He declared for the NBA draft after his junior year, but he was not one of the sixty players selected.

That first year I coached the Energy, we were hovering around the .500 mark and trying to sell tickets. We already had three Iowa guys on our team, and Curtis, who was still well known in the state, became available. He had already kicked around, having played briefly for clubs in Greece and Croatia, a couple of NBA Summer League teams, and four different D-League teams.

That may sound like a ridiculous amount of team-hopping but it's not all that unusual for players in basketball's minor leagues. They keep looking for better opportunities—a little more money, maybe what seems like a more likely entry point to the NBA— and they either jump to the next team, or the one they're with finds them expendable. (My basketball résumé looked pretty crazy, too, before I joined the Raptors.)

I only had Curtis for seven games at the end of that first season, but I noticed something in him. When the ball was on the floor, there could be five guys rolling around trying to get it, but he'd be the one to come up with it. He was built like a full-back, six foot three and about 215 pounds, and he played with an incredible toughness.

I knew he had been on a whirlwind and I figured he might benefit from some stability, and if I gave him a featured role, maybe that would be the best thing for his long-term goals. "You ought to come back here next year," I told him. "Forget about going overseas. I'm going to put the basketball in your hands and it's going to be your team to run."

He really liked that suggestion, and he came back. And he

stayed. For the next three seasons, 165 straight games, we were in first place.

We'd have a bunch of guys called up, or maybe one go to Europe, or we'd make a trade, and the next thing you knew it was Curtis and four new guys out there. And I'd say to them, "It would be a really good idea if you went over there and made friends with him. He's going to determine where the ball goes, and if you've got a decent relationship with him, he's probably going to get you your twenty-five points a night. And if you don't, he's going to make sure you don't."

I didn't mean they had to be best buddies with Curtis, and that's not what he wanted. What I was trying to convey was that they had to be good citizens on the court—play the right way—and he would help them meet their individual goals.

Curtis was not unlike Kyle Lowry, who is now in his eighth season running the point with the Raptors. Curtis could be a little moody at times, but he was also strong-willed and smart as hell.

A basketball season is long, and it involves a small group of players traveling together, working in close quarters, and trying to pull in the same direction about four times a week in high-pressure situations. Guys get upset. They make it known.

With players like Curtis, and like Kyle now, I want their teammates to care about keeping them happy because those are the guys who really know how to play basketball. What they're demanding of the others is generally going to be the right thing.

⌃

In 2011, the year we won the D-League championship, our opponent in the final, best-of-three series was the Rio Grande

Valley Vipers. In the first game, which we won on the road, Curtis had a triple-double—twenty-nine points, ten rebounds, and ten assists. In our first home game, an incredible night in a sold-out Wells Fargo Arena, he had another triple-double.

He had averaged nineteen points a game during the regular season and just a shade under ten assists and was the D-League's MVP.

Curtis is still living in Iowa—he's got a son, Curtis Jr., and is coaching AAU ball—but he never got called up by the NBA, and that may be the biggest regret of my career. A couple of different times, I thought, *This is the moment. A team has a need for a point guard and he's the perfect guy.*

I pleaded with a few teams to just give him one shot. I was trying hard to make it happen so he would have a chance to show himself. I wanted some NBA team to see what I did. At the very least, I wanted Curtis to be able to say he put on an NBA jersey, even if it was only for ten days.

7

HOOPS LAB IN THE RIO GRANDE

DISRUPTION ON THE HARDWOOD

Demonstrating proper shooting technique with the Nurse's Pill.

(Nurse family collection)

After four years with the Iowa Energy, I still had one more stop before entering the NBA. In 2011, I became the head coach of another D-League team, the Rio Grande Valley Vipers. It may have looked like a lateral move, just another station on the minor-league circuit, but I went because the Vipers were unlike any other team in the D-League—or really, any team anywhere.

Two years before, the NBA's Houston Rockets had entered into an agreement in which the Vipers would remain under local ownership while the Rockets brain trust ran the basketball operation. Their idea was to use the team in the same way a corporation makes use of its research and development department. Specifically, the Rockets wanted to experiment with how fast a team could play—and how many three-point shots it could launch.

When the NBA introduced the three-pointer in 1979, some disliked it just on principle. "We don't need it. I say leave our game alone," said legendary Celtics coach Red Auerbach, by then retired. John MacLeod, who was coaching the Phoenix Suns, said, "It may change our game at the end of quarters. But I'm not going to set up plays for guys to bomb from twenty-three feet. I think that's very boring basketball."

Even the coaches who did not express some personal dislike of the three-pointer took a long time coming around to its tactical and mathematical advantages. In that first season, just 3 percent of the shots attempted league-wide were from behind the arc. In the 1980 Finals, between the Lakers and 76ers, the teams combined to make just one three-point shot. *One.* Over the course of six games.

And by the way, it wasn't like the NBA didn't have players who were great shooters. The league back then included Larry Bird, George Gervin, Jim Paxson, Calvin Murphy, and even "Downtown" Freddie Brown—whose reputation and nickname for long-range shooting did not come from attempting a high volume of three-pointers. All those guys could have shot a lot of three-pointers and made a good percentage; they just didn't.

"Downtown" took eighty-eight three-pointers that first season, or about one a game, which was a lot back in the day. But his high percentage, 44 percent, indicated he should have attempted a lot more of them.

By the time the Rockets took over the Vipers, the NBA had come a long way in its thinking. Six teams in 2009 averaged more than twenty three-point attempts a game; the league leader, the New York Knicks, put up just shy of twenty-eight a game.

Daryl Morey, the Houston Rockets general manager, understood what may now seem like the obvious advantages of the shot—it is worth one point more!—and the logic of why teams should devise systems to get more long-range opportunities.

The first coach he hired to test this out was Chris Finch, who had a background a whole lot like mine. He played in England and then coached in England, Germany, and Belgium. We coached against each other in the BBL and were bitter adversaries. He was at Sheffield the whole time, and wherever I happened to be coaching, it seemed like I was duking it out with him at every turn.

We eventually became good friends, and I was his assistant when he served as head coach of the British team in the 2012 Olympics in London.

Chris spent two years leading the Vipers. When he left to become an assistant coach with the Rockets, I came in to replace him. It might seem like a coincidence that we had traveled the same path and then both ended up in the same job down in the Rio Grande Valley, but I'd say it probably was not.

I think we both spent so much time far off the radar, in settings with odd assemblages of talent and players of all shapes and sizes—where we might end up, say, playing with four guards and no center—that we were good candidates to preside over what's been described as a basketball laboratory. We had already spent years figuring it out as we went along.

⌃

In a 2014 story for *Texas Monthly* magazine, a Rockets executive explained the usefulness of the Vipers to the big club: "There's certain basketball factors that you can't evaluate at the NBA level, because it's going to cost you wins and losses," he said. "But at the D-League level, you can experiment, you can try things, you can see the results and then apply it [in the NBA]."

The Rockets are a metrics-based organization, so they understood what they were getting when they offered me the job. They had crunched the numbers on my coaching style from Europe and the D-League and knew my teams spread the floor and played fast. I was already aligned with what they were seeking.

Chris Finch, a really good basketball man who is now the associate head coach with the New Orleans Pelicans, had won a D-League championship with the Vipers. He had the team taking a ton of three-pointers. I built on what he had started, and I codified the offensive system and gave it a name: the shot spectrum.

Here's what that meant: we assigned value to every potential shot. The highest was a drive to the basket that resulted in a foul and two free throws. (Or even better yet: a made basket as well as a free throw, though a lot of times in the NBA an opponent is going to foul you hard enough that you won't make the shot.) That's the best offensive move in basketball—you should get two or three points out of it, and you get the other team in foul trouble, increasing the chances they reach their foul limit in a quarter and you get even more foul shots. (Drawing a foul is basically a multiplier.)

The second-highest-valued shot is one right at the rim. A layup or dunk.

Then comes a three-point attempt from the corner. The distance from there on an NBA court is only twenty-two feet, as opposed to 23.75 feet from the top of the arc—which may not seem like much, but it makes a big difference in the percentage that players shoot. After that comes an open look from elsewhere beyond the arc, even if it's not from the corner.

The most crucial aspect of the shot spectrum is the shot I do *not* want you to take—the midrange jump shot or floater from outside the painted area, but inside the three-point arc. This is sometimes called the "tough two."

Some of the game's greatest players—Michael Jordan, the late Kobe Bryant, Dirk Nowitzki—excelled at making these midrange shots, even when they were closely guarded. If you look at a Jordan highlight reel, it's all you will see (other than the flying dunks)—twelve-foot jump shots with defenders draped all over him.

He made those shots, but normal players do not shoot them nearly as well—in fact, their typical percentage is in the mid– or upper–30 percent range. So why would you take that shot if you could get an open three-point shot?

Well, you shouldn't. Even if you make 50 percent of your two-pointers—which is hard to do if you're taking tough ones—you end up with one hundred points on one hundred attempts (fifty made shots). Thirty-five percent of one hundred three-pointers gets you 105 points.

The NBA is filled with guys who can hit 35 percent of their three-point attempts. The best shooters do better than that. The idea is to design an offense that maximizes opportunities for good shooters to get those three-point shots.

It's math and it's not all that complicated. The whole logic behind the shot spectrum is that the tough two is basketball poison—to be avoided at all costs. That is accepted wisdom now, but it was less so in 2011 when I started with the Vipers.

My work in the Rio Grande Valley was a next step, an advancement in my longtime interest in shooting. Now, instead of just teaching players how to shoot correctly, I was intensely focused on *where* they should shoot from—what spots on the floor.

I found a structured way to teach the shot spectrum. I put Xs all over the Vipers practice floor that marked where we wanted to take our shots. Different values were assigned to each one.

When we scrimmaged, I gave an extra point to a corner three—it was a four-pointer. I subtracted points when any of our players attempted a long two-point shot. I wanted to drill home the point: Why take a twenty-one-footer, probably with a guy hanging all over you, if you could find open space outside the arc and shoot for three?

We'd go three-on-three and the only thing our players were allowed to do was run to the rim or shoot a corner three. We eliminated the whole rest of the court. Even at the start of practice, as the players were loosening up, they were not allowed to shoot from the forbidden areas.

It was hard for them at first. They had spent their whole careers to that point working on pretty little turnaround twelve-footers—the Jordan shots. The Dirk Nowitzki special. Kobe Bryant was a big NBA star at the time and those were the shots he was taking.

I had guys say to me, "Coach, man, my whole game is the seventeen-foot pull-up," and I'd respond, "Not anymore. Not anymore it's not." In games, I'd call a time-out after a player took one of the forbidden shots and say to him, "You understand that I'm serious about this? We're not shooting that shot anymore."

Before too long, our players got used to what I was asking of them, and they even started policing themselves. I barely had to say anything. If one of them launched from the forbidden area, you'd hear somebody shout: That's not our shot! In games, we were shooting something like 4 percent non-paint twos, which was the lowest, by far, in pro basketball.

It's one thing to want to take quality three-point shots and another to devise an offense where you can get them. That is even more true when nearly everyone sees the value of them.

Most defenses now are basically the inverse of the offense we worked on with the Vipers. They want to funnel you into the exact areas where you do not want to take your shots from.

Defenders run players off the three-point line—by either closely guarding them, or by flying at them as they are about to launch a shot. If the offensive man goes by the defender, his teammates, playing "help" defense, want to corral the player in that midrange area where he has no choice other than attempting a closely defended two-point shot.

(In more traditional basketball, you always wanted to stay in front of your man. That was the cardinal rule, and it still applies on certain parts of the court. But it is no longer a defensive sin if your guy gets around because you have prevented him from taking an open three-pointer—and in doing so, induced him into taking a twelve-foot shot.)

Our offense with the Vipers bears similarities to what I run now with the Raptors. We drove the ball hard to the basket and if we couldn't get a foul or layup, we kicked it to the corner if we could—or to a teammate at the top of the arc. We set picks, we drove it again and kicked it out, we reversed the ball from side to side. We wanted to play with continuity and with some beauty.

One thing I've tried to do in this book is connect some dots and show how my journey has led to what I do now in the NBA. Looking back at my time in the D-League, and before that to my years in England, I can see that my willingness to be inventive became a habit. It expanded my imagination.

I am going to jump way ahead for a moment. In early December of 2019, the Houston Rockets came in to play us in Toronto. Their coach, Mike D'Antoni, is one of the game's great innovators. (He also began his coaching career outside the US, spending seven years leading teams in Italy after first playing for a dozen years over there.)

Before that game, I hinted that I might do something special against James Harden, who can be difficult to guard one-on-one. In fact, basically no one can guard Harden. If you give him a little space, he nails a three. If you get too close, he either drives by you and gets all the way to the rim—or he leans in from beyond the arc and draws a foul.

He has a way of raising up for a shot from underneath a defender's outstretched hands that consistently gets him free throws. If I were to be mildly critical, I'd say that he has conditioned refs to give him that call. It is highly effective for him—and incredibly frustrating for his opponents. (In 2019–20 he leads the league in foul shot attempts—averaging twelve a game, almost two more than the next-highest player on the list.)

When the Rockets came into Toronto in the first week in December, he was averaging nearly thirty-nine points a game. If you want to know how unusual that is, no one has ended a season with an average that high since Wilt Chamberlain in 1963.

I sort of teased my plan to put something in the Rockets' heads. "We've got an idea of something we're gonna try and we'll see if we have enough guts to go with it," I told reporters.

Well, I did have the guts to do it, although after the game there seemed to be some questions around how smart it was. One of our defenders stayed with Harden—and every time he got the ball in his hands, we sent another player at him—usually Fred VanVleet.

It was basically a zone defense, a modification of a box-in-one. I called it a diamond and one. Fred was at the top of the diamond and as soon as Harden touched the ball, he doubled him.

But Harden was really smart. He didn't force anything—he just gave the ball up when our two defenders hemmed him in and allowed his teammates to play against us four-on-three.

We did a good job and got a lot of deflections—forty-one total for the game—but the ball caromed their way a lot. They took fifty-five three-point attempts, some of them wide open from the corner, and made 40 percent of them. When they missed shots, our defenders, who were scrambling around trying to guard open players, had a hard time getting back into rebounding position and we gave up too many second chances.

Afterward, the reporters kept asking me if I had considered coming out of that defense. I said yes, I did, but it was an interesting experiment to see play out. And I wanted to see it for forty-eight minutes rather than bailing on it at the end. It wasn't great, but it was pretty good—and would have been even better if we could have rebounded more of the missed shots we created.

The players embraced the experiment. You can't tinker around without their being willing to try something different, and not all players are. But I think our roster is naturally inclined in that direction. They have seen that while our experiments don't always work, they do always teach us something.

I came in at halftime and said, "I don't know, guys, what do you think?" And they were all like, "Come on. Let's stay in it."

Harden only scored twenty-three points, but his teammates killed us. We had been holding teams to 106 points a game, but the Rockets beat us 119–106.

That's how coaching is sometimes. You try to win every game, but the NBA regular season is long—eighty-two games from late October through mid-April. To experiment along the way can be a little fun, but mostly it's useful—a part of a long intelligence-gathering operation. Who are your best players? How do you put them in positions to succeed? And how do you defend the other teams' great players?

You're always probing, seeking more information.

⌃

Rio Grande was important in opening up my mind and freeing me to experiment. I never had an uncomfortable moment with the organization. That's unusual. If we ever lost a few games in a row, they would quickly say, "Stick with it. We like what you're doing."

They were clear about their order of priorities. They wanted me to develop their guys, meaning always have one or two ready that could hit the court for the big club.

Use the place as a laboratory. Basically, just tinker. Throw a lot of stuff out there and see what you can discover.

And third, win some games for the community. We played a couple of miles from the Mexican border. It was a whole different vibe, different food, different music. I really enjoyed it—it felt like I was coaching in Europe again in that I was enveloped in some other culture.

And the cool thing is, we did win. The first year, my experiments did not result in enough victories and we didn't even make the playoffs. But in year two, we finished 35-15 and ripped through three rounds of postseason series without a defeat.

I had the MVP of the league on my roster for most of the season, Andrew Goudelock, a six-foot-three guard from the College of Charleston who had already had a little taste of the NBA. We got him in a classic kind of D-League transaction. Andrew was a little temperamental and we had heard he was not getting along with his coach in Sioux Falls. But by the standards of the league, he was a stud, and I really wanted to get him.

We acquired him in a three-way trade that also brought us a player named Mike Singletary Jr., who was a very solidly built forward. (We all assumed for weeks that he was the son of the Hall of Fame Chicago Bears linebacker of the same name until someone asked how his dad was and he said that he was still teaching high school.)

Goudelock played great for us—so well that by the time our

playoffs started, he had been called up by the Lakers. He even started a couple of playoff games for them. (He is now a seven-figure player in Europe.)

The team we defeated in the Finals was Santa Cruz, and after the clinching game, I shook hands with their head coach—Nate Bjorkgren, my former assistant with the Iowa Energy and the guy I spent that summer with drawing up plays in my basement.

It was a great moment. My relationship with Nate went all the way back to the University of South Dakota, when I was an assistant coach in my early twenties and he was a freshman point guard. And though I had no way of knowing it at the time, Nate had first become aware of me even before that. When he was ten years old, he was in the stands at Veterans Memorial Auditorium, with his dad, when my Kuemper Catholic team won the Iowa state championship.

As we embraced at half-court together after the D-League championship game, I said to him, "You know what, Nate? I think you and I could both do this at a higher level."

8

TORONTO

PUTTING WHAT I THOUGHT I KNEW TO THE TEST

With Kyle Lowry at a game at Boston's TD Garden. *(Adam Glanzman / Getty Images)*

The championship season with the Rio Grande Valley Vipers was my twenty-fourth year of coaching and my twentieth as a head coach. I was forty-six years old and had coached well over a thousand games, all of them below the NBA level. I wouldn't say, necessarily, that I was running out of time, but I was a long way from where I started—no longer the prodigy who was the youngest coach in England, the youngest in the NCAA, the youngest in Belgium. I had been at it for a while and I was eager for a team in the league to give me a chance—which I knew would come, if it did at all, as an assistant.

NBA teams frequently scout my D-League games, looking for players to add to their rosters. But at one point in my 2012–13 season with the Vipers, a Raptors scout (or sometimes two) watched our team play for more than a month straight, about fifteen games total. That was unusual. After I kept seeing their people showing up, I figured that they had taken an interest in our innovative style of play—and might even be scouting me for a job on their bench.

It made sense for them to be looking to make changes. Toronto came into the NBA in 1995 and had a good, energized fan base, but over the years experienced only modest on-court success.

In their first eighteen seasons, they qualified for the playoffs just five times and, when they did get in, didn't do very well. They won a first-round playoff series in 2001; the other years they qualified, they got knocked out in the first round. By 2013, it had been six years since the Raptors ended a season with a winning record.

That spring, after both the Vipers and Raptors finished playing, I got a call from Bryan Colangelo, the team's general manager, asking me to come to Toronto and talk with them. I flew up there and met with Colangelo, another Raptors executive, Ed Stefanski, and the team's head coach, Dwane Casey. They sat me down in a meeting room lined with dry-erase boards and, after some pleasantries in the first few minutes, threw me a marker and basically said, "Show us how you run your offense."

I got up and just started wheeling and dealing. I showed them what we do when we're coming down on a fast break—and then how we initiate the offense in the half-court.

I paid a lot of attention to how we played when the twenty-four-second shot clock gets into single digits, which is a challenge for all teams. The tendency is for everyone to just stop. You've run your offense and it hasn't produced a good shot so the player left with the ball goes one-on-one. I've tried to design offenses that do not go static—that keep cycling through to the end with screen setting and ball and player movement so we're left with something better than a desperation heave.

I put the shot spectrum up on the whiteboards. I drew the Xs and showed them how we teach it. I highlighted the areas of the court where the tough twos come from—the midrange shots that should be the last option.

They asked me questions about how I teach certain things and I drew more stuff up on the boards. They asked me how I thought stuff might have to be modified for the NBA, and I answered them as I drew some more with the marker.

I'm sure I could've looked like a madman, but let's face it,

I knew the material, I was passionate about it, and I had been waiting for a long time to show it to someone in the NBA.

My interview (or performance) got me a job offer. But it ended up not going as smoothly as I had hoped. Of course it didn't.

Before I left Toronto, Colangelo offered me a job to serve as an assistant on Dwane Casey's staff. A three-year deal for something like $1.2 million, so $400,000 a year. I was making $100,000 with the Vipers. I was like, holy shit, yeah, I'll take it. (I was between agents at the time, so I just handled it myself.)

This was on a Sunday or Monday, and Colangelo said there was just one small thing: his own contract was rolling over on that coming Wednesday and he couldn't do any new business before then. All I had to do was hang on for a couple of days and he would send me the paperwork to finalize the deal.

Well, Wednesday rolls around and they fire Colangelo. I don't have a job offer anymore.

At that point, I could have joined the Houston Rockets staff. Their offer was for less money than Toronto had offered, but that's not what kept me from accepting. If I took it, I would have been pretty far down the ladder among the assistants and my seat would have been behind the bench, not on it, during games. It was clear that the Raptors had wanted me to have a strong voice in how they played, and that was what I wanted—to see how my thinking would play out in the NBA.

What happened next was that Dwane Casey kept his job but just about everybody else in the basketball operation got fired, including his assistants. It was a big shake-up. Dwane and I kept talking, and he assured me he still wanted me on his staff.

Colangelo's replacement in Toronto was Masai Ujiri, whom I coached against when he was playing professionally in England. About six weeks after the first Toronto offer fell through, I was hired onto Casey's staff, though just on a one-year deal.

I immediately asked Dwane who was coaching the Raptors' Summer League team in Las Vegas, their roster of rookies and free agents. I knew they probably didn't have anybody since most of his staff had been let go. It was just about to start, and he was going to do it himself, which is not something head coaches normally do. (They stop in and observe.) I told him I would do it for him if he wanted me to.

My go-to at that moment, as always, was just to coach. The whole hiring thing had been a mess—there was certainly some anxiety involved—so I just figured let me go out there and get to work.

The next day, I was on a plane to Vegas. I checked in to my hotel and then headed to the high school gym where the Raptors' summer team was practicing. Masai showed up with a contract—we went into an office and he laid it down on a desk and I signed it, and then I went out to the gym, blew the whistle, and we started practicing.

⌃

In September 2013, my first season as an NBA assistant, the Raptors gathered for preseason training camp in Halifax, Nova Scotia. At our second practice, I was running an offensive drill and two different guys tossed me a ball. I didn't see the one coming and it smashed my glasses. I just chucked them to the side and kept on rolling. I could still see, though not perfectly.

It was purely an accident, but the players were laughing about it and I didn't want to allow it to become a big joke by stopping the drill and trying to repair them or by putting back on a pair of busted glasses. That may seem humorless on my part, but the thing you have to understand is that a new coach in the NBA is on trial.

If you've played sports at a lower level, you may remember that a lot of your energy went into trying to impress your coach. If you wanted to play, you had to make him love you. That gets inverted in the NBA. A new coach—especially an assistant up from the D-League with zero playing pedigree—has to impress the players. He has to sell himself.

What are you bringing that can improve the team? Uplift their individual games? Better their position in the marketplace?

If you try to tell them about the championships you won with the Iowa Energy or Rio Grande Valley Vipers (or, God forbid, the titles in England), you're making a big mistake. A couple of guys on the roster might be able to relate, but it won't mean a thing to the team's top players and they'll just laugh at you.

(One quick aside about the glasses: I went to an eye doctor the next day in Halifax and got new ones. That off-season, I got LASIK surgery, so I don't need them anymore. The season came around and after the first game, I saw that I'd received several calls from my mom.

When I reached back out to her, she said, "How come you weren't on the bench tonight?" I told her I got that surgery and I was there, but without glasses. She said to me, "You put those glasses back on. I can't find you on TV."

So I did. I put on glasses with clear lenses. My mom passed away in 2019, while we were on a West Coast road trip, at ninety-four, but I'm still wearing them.)

The Raptors were not my team to run and I was not asked to install my offense wholesale. I was working with what existed— still a lot of set plays—and trying to improve the beginning and the end of those sets. We wanted to be able to take advantage of opportunities when the play broke down—to set some random screens and continue to play.

I taught a version of the shot spectrum and tried to get us away from taking as many midrange jump shots. But that was a hard sell. A first-year assistant coach can only have limited influence in breaking players' lifelong habits. Our top scorer was DeMar DeRozan, who had made a really good living off midrange shots and was not about to stop shooting them just because I showed up.

Right from the start, I was running film sessions. These are critiques—in training camp, of practices—and once the season gets started, of both games and practices.

I'll admit that I was nervous in the beginning in front of that group. The players will test you. They'll give you shit if you put something up on the board and you make a mistake, even if you just misspell a word. Don't get me wrong. They are rooting for you, not against you—players in the NBA definitely want to be coached—but it's a tough crowd. You need to connect with them and do it quickly.

You edit the film to show a limited number of plays—you don't want everyone sitting in the film room forever—but you need to be in there long enough to correct mistakes. If a guy cut right when he should have gone left, you show him. If he jacked up his own shot instead of passing to an open teammate with a better opportunity, you point that out.

You try to ask questions so it's not a monologue. If it was an end-of-game situation and we got one of our players what seemed like a good shot, but he missed it, you might ask: Is that where you want to receive the ball?

It can be fairly subtle. A teammate may have tried to get it to him in a slightly different position but could not get the right passing angle. So you might talk about a slight adjustment to improve the passing angle.

Basketball is on one level about geometry. The good players understand that and will get into discussions about slight tweaks of how we're setting screens, making passes, or running to certain spots on the floor. The guys who do not care about that level of detail are the ones who quickly wash out of the league.

There can always be some discomfort with film sessions, and you have to mix in plenty of praise with the criticism. And it's certainly harder when you're a new assistant coach. You know they're looking at you and thinking: Who is this guy? He came to us from where again?

As a coach in this situation, you have to address their mistakes. If you're timid about it, you lose respect. But you have to be right, and you have a short time to prove that you know what you're talking about.

There were several tricky aspects to that first season in Toronto. One was that for the first time in almost two decades, I was not a head coach. I was serving on a staff with four other assistants. The last time I had been in that position was 1995, in Vermillion, South Dakota, when I worked under head coach Dave Boots.

I wanted my voice to be heard, and I was brought in there

to introduce some new concepts. But I didn't know the other coaches before we got there. We are all new, except for the head coach, Dwane Casey, and everybody had their own careers to tend to and their own ambitions.

A lot of what I was working through was the normal stuff anybody has to figure out in a new workplace. When do you speak up at meetings? How much do you talk? When is it okay for me to go into the head coach's office and talk with him privately?

All of this goes back to Mudra. Everyone is going to have their own personal agenda in addition to a team agenda, and they are going to put some thought and energy into each of those considerations. It's unrealistic to think otherwise. I was not the only one hoping to advance my career and possibly become a head coach one day.

But to be honest, I did not have a lot of practice at this kind of in-office diplomacy. It's one of the things I missed out on, having gone away and become a head coach at such a young age, and then being the guy in charge when I came to the D-League. I just went on my best instincts and fell back on the normal human qualities I learned back in Iowa: Try not to be a jerk. Be decent to other people and let them have a say, but don't hide your own light under a bushel.

There was one huge thing that we were all dealing with together: all of us, including Dwane Casey, were on a short leash.

Dwane had one year left on his three-year contract when Masai Ujiri took over for Bryan Colangelo. He spared Dwane when he cleaned house, but he did not extend his contract. And when I signed my deal to be one of the assistants, after my initial three-year offer fell through, I was told that nobody was getting anything but a one-year contract.

The message was clear enough: the team had to improve or

we were all going to be quickly out on our asses. They made just a one-year investment in us for a reason. I don't know that any of us really verbalized it with one another. We may have here or there, but it was well understood—we were on probation.

NBA coaching jobs are hard to get. I was proof of that. But as hard as it is to get into the league, it can be even harder to get back into it if you lose a job—especially if you've only had it for a year or two.

There's a long line of people wanting those jobs—assistant college coaches, NBA scouts, former players, former head coaches who got fired. If you get fired before you've accomplished anything, you can get sent back to the end of a long line and maybe never find your way back. I know coaches who that has happened to.

The Raptors had finished 34-48 the year before I started as an assistant, an improvement over their previous season but their fifth straight year of not qualifying for the playoffs. None of us knew what the benchmark was for keeping our jobs, but we knew we had to do a hell of a lot better than that.

About six weeks into that season, it wasn't looking good at all. We started out all right, but then went into a nosedive, losing five straight games starting Thanksgiving week and continuing into early December.

Our record stood at 6-12. Several of our losses went right down to the wire—we lost two overtime games on the road, one of them in double overtime—but I didn't figure we were going to get any credit for that. Maybe just the opposite: sometimes when a team loses by just a bucket or two, people figure there was probably something the coaches could have done to get a different result.

On December 8, our front office made a trade. It wasn't the kind of deal that shakes up the NBA or gets the lead spot on ESPN's *SportsCenter.*

The centerpiece of the deal was Rudy Gay, whom we sent to the Sacramento Kings. Rudy was our second-leading scorer and had been with us for less than a year. We got him in the middle of the previous season in a trade with Memphis.

He was making big money, nearly $18 million a year, which is often a factor in NBA trades. (Complicated considerations over money and "clearing payroll" to get teams into line with the salary cap—or well under the cap in order to make room for future deals—are behind many NBA trades.)

There were six others involved in the trade, most of whom would be considered NBA journeymen. In addition to Gay, we sent the Kings Aaron Gray and Quincy Acy. The four players we got in return were John Salmons, Greivis Vásquez, Patrick Patterson, and Chuck Hayes.

Salmons had once been a nearly twenty-point-a-game scorer, but he was thirty-four years old and it looked like his career was winding down. The others were solid players, the types whom coaches counted on to play fifteen minutes or so a game and either give the team a spark or hold the fort until the starters returned.

You would not have predicted it, but this trade totally turned our team around. All of a sudden, we had a bench and some chemistry. Our talent level had not increased much (if at all), but the guys we assembled liked playing together and they started clicking.

From the day of the trade until the end of the regular season, we won forty-two of our remaining sixty-four games and finished with a record of 48-34. We finished first in our division and earned the third seed in the conference going into the playoffs.

And I'm pretty sure we saved our jobs.

You really couldn't have predicted any of it. I don't know that our front office, the executives who made the trade, would have seen it coming.

We don't have any of those players we got from the Kings anymore—Patrick Patterson stayed the longest, another three seasons—but the deal was the beginning of some good things.

In my first year as a Raptors assistant, that 2013–14 season when the team started to turn things around, we were matched up against the Brooklyn Nets in the first round of the playoffs. We had four more wins than they did in the regular season, earning us the higher seed and the home court advantage in a seven-game series.

I have no idea what the Las Vegas odds were, but I'm sure that a lot of smart basketball people believed the Nets would win. There was even a perception that the Nets "mailed in the last few games of the regular season," as a writer for ESPN put it, in order to make sure we were their first-round opponent.

The average age of their starting lineup was thirty-three. Ours was twenty-four. Our most experienced player, Kyle Lowry, was twenty-seven and playing alongside a twenty-one-year-old (Jonas Valančiūnas) and a twenty-two-year-old (Terrence Ross). The contrast in the experience levels was about as stark as you'll ever see, and while it didn't predetermine the result, it was something for us to overcome.

If you watch the NBA casually, it can seem like a young man's league. Players are flying around and dunking and doing all kinds of acrobatic-looking things.

But when the games count the most, in the postseason, it looks a little different. The defense is tighter and the pace usually slower. It's more of a half-court game. More cerebral.

It's still exciting—even more so because the stakes are higher—but the playoffs, more times than not, are when teams with young stars lose out to ones led by older, more experienced players. The veterans have a savvy that the younger guys lack. They know how games are going to be officiated and they tend to have a little more poise at the end.

One of the other big advantages the older players have is something that may surprise fans: a lot of the younger ones do not know how hard they have to fight in the postseason. How intense and focused they have to be in every single possession, every trip down the floor.

The level of effort required, both mental and physical, is un-imaginable to them until they've been through it, and sometimes they have to lose—multiple times—to finally understand what's required. It's true for just about every player, and very rarely are there shortcuts. Young players do win championships, but almost never when they are the stars, the ones carrying the load. It usually happens when they are on teams led by a veteran All-Star or two.

LeBron James entered the NBA at age nineteen but did not win a title until he was twenty-seven and in his ninth season in the league—and after his teams had twice reached the NBA Finals and lost. It was not all on him, of course, and his teams in Cleveland probably did not have enough talent surrounding him. But he did not win it all until he signed with Miami and was paired with Dwyane Wade, who was three years older and already had an NBA title on his résumé. The other key component on that team was Chris Bosh, a former Raptor.

Michael Jordan won his first title when he was in his seventh season. Like LeBron, he was twenty-seven. His teams were knocked out of the playoffs three times by the Detroit Pistons, who had an older roster led by veterans Isiah Thomas, Bill Laimbeer, and Rick Mahorn.

The 2008 NBA champion Boston Celtics were an extreme example of how age and experience often rule the NBA postseason. The Celtics' top three scorers were Paul Pierce (who was thirty years old), Kevin Garnett (thirty-one), and Ray Allen (thirty-two). Two of their key players off the bench, Sam Cassell and PJ Brown, were both thirty-eight.

Those are ages you associate with people becoming surgeons, or school principals, or ascending to some high rank in the military—and not with playing in the NBA and competing against guys with forty-inch vertical leaping ability.

︿

Kevin Garnett and Paul Pierce, graybeards on that Celtics championship team, were with the Nets team that we took on in the spring of 2014. Pierce was the young man, at thirty-six. Garnett was a year older. They had two other players in their mid-thirties, Jason Terry and Jason Collins.

In the first game, we played from behind almost all night, briefly took a lead with about five minutes left, and then ended up losing, 94–87. The defeat immediately squandered our home court advantage—the start of what would become an unfortunate pattern in the coming years.

From there, the series was a back-and-forth fight, with almost all the games close. We went into the fifth game of the series, again at home, tied at two games each.

We came out flying and had a twenty-six-point lead early in the second half, and by the end of the third quarter, still led by twenty-two. At that point, we unraveled quickly. We bricked long jump shots. We missed two-foot layup attempts. We threw the ball to the other team.

The game was tied, 101–101, with three minutes left. What saved us was Kyle Lowry, who had thirty-six points for the night. He hit a three-point jump shot with about a minute left to give us the lead back, and we ended up winning, 115–113, when a Nets player blew their final chance by throwing a pass over a teammate's head.

We then lost the next game in Brooklyn and came home for the deciding Game 7. It was a crazy day in Toronto. Lots of buzz over our game, plus a marathon going through the downtown streets. The city was so gridlocked that Dwane Casey started out in his car for the arena, got stopped in traffic, and then had to turn around and take the subway to the game.

We began badly. Brooklyn had the lead almost the whole night, and we were still down nine points with three minutes left before we finally rallied. With eight seconds left, Terrence Ross hit a layup to close their lead to 104–103.

One second later, as they tried to inbound after Terrence's basket, we stole the ball. It was a great play. Terrence stepped in and grabbed the ball and then, just as he was about to step out of bounds, fired it off Pierce and over the end line. That gave us 6.2 seconds, plenty of time to set up a play, score a basket, and win the series.

Remember I wrote that it is not as easy as it looks to draw up plays at the end of games in loud arenas? This was all of that and more: a huge decibel level, a young team in the huddle, and a season on the line.

It is fair to say that we had some anxiety and also a little bit of confusion. We were inbounding at half-court, from the right sideline, after another assistant coach checked with the officials and initially said the ball was coming in from the other side. The refs may have made a mistake, or it might just have been so damn loud in there he didn't hear what they said correctly. But we had set up a play for what was basically the mirror image of what we had to run.

We wanted to get the ball to Kyle Lowry in the center of the court, the obvious move, and let him operate one-on-one and get himself a shot or quickly find an open teammate. And we didn't want anyone to come up and set a screen for him, fearing the Nets would trap him if that happened.

But a teammate did come up and try to free him with a pick and it all descended from there. Believe me, you wouldn't want to see a video of it.

Kyle dribbled to his left and managed to get into the lane— he kept control of the ball when it almost squirted away—but he was swarmed by four defenders. With his last dribble he launched himself right into the chest of thirty-six-year-old Paul Pierce, who rose up and blocked the shot.

Pierce had not done much the whole game—and who knows how many games it had been since he blocked a shot—but he made that play. And that was the end. Game over, series over.

Nobody likes to lose, and it did sting that night, but it didn't feel super tragic. It was totally unexpected that we were in the playoffs at all. We took them to seven games. We kind of maxed out. The team grew up and it was a hell of a year.

And after starting the season knowing that our heads were all on the chopping block, we survived. Management was happy. They were, like, okay, you guys did great and we're going to do everything we can to make the team a little better. And by the way, here's a new three-year contract for everybody.

That was a good feeling for me. I had been in the job market just about every off-season for my whole career, either because I wanted to get somewhere better, or my team over in England got sold—or it ran out of money and was spiraling toward bankruptcy—or some other crazy thing was coming down the line that suggested to me that it would be a good idea to move on.

I had gotten used to all of that, but all I ever really wanted was a chance to coach and get better at it. I didn't have anything *against* stability. Now, after a year in the NBA, it looked like I would get to stay for at least a little while.

︿

Pressure to win is a constant in professional sports. If it ever seems to lift, just for a bit, in some rebuilding year or a season or series you are not "supposed" to win, it quickly comes roaring back. It probably even builds up a little steam while you thought it was lying dormant.

We had another good regular season in 2014–15, finishing with a 49-33 record. That was one victory better than the previous year. And then we had a brutal postseason.

Our opponent in the first round was the Washington Wizards. We had home court advantage again. And we got blitzed. We lost four straight games.

The first one close. We fell way behind early, came back, and then lost in overtime. (Our old friend, the ageless Paul Pierce, who had signed with the Wizards as a free agent in the off-season, led them with twenty points.)

The second game was not particularly competitive, the third game we hung with them most of the way before folding at the end, and Game 4 was just embarrassing. We trailed by fourteen points by the end of the first quarter and it just kept getting worse. By midway through the fourth quarter, we were losing by thirty-seven.

The final score was 125-94. After a season that rolled on for six months, we washed out of the playoffs in eight days.

Normally, when the season ends everybody just takes off for a while. You go home, rest up, sleep in, go on vacation with your family. But the Raptors management told us nobody was going anywhere—to plan on staying in Toronto for at least a week.

We had meetings in a fifteenth-floor conference room at the team's downtown headquarters. Masai Ujiri, the team president, presided over them and was joined by Jeff Weltman, our general manager, who later became the president of the Orlando Magic, and Bobby Webster, who was the Raptors assistant general manager and eventually GM.

The coaches were really on the firing line. They asked how we scored so efficiently during the regular season and then looked like we were stuck in mud for four straight games in the playoffs.

What happened to our defense? What happened to our chemistry? What about the first game, the one that went to overtime? How did we come back so hard to tie the game and then revert in the OT session to the same crap that caused us to fall behind early in the game?

And that fourth game, when we got blown out? How the hell did that happen? How did we feel about that? (Uh, we felt bad about it. What would you think?)

The questions were entirely legitimate. But as you might imagine, it was unpleasant. It was almost torture. There was no back-patting about what a nice regular season we had, nor should there have been. You play those eighty-two games to get into the playoffs, to get a decent seed, and to develop a competitive, cohesive squad that can compete for a championship.

What your fans (and management) care about is what you did in the playoffs. In that same 2014–15 season, the Atlanta Hawks had a really nice team—no superstars, but balanced scoring led by Paul Millsap, Kyle Korver, DeMarre Carroll, and Al Horford.

But I don't know how many people would remember that squad. Outside of Atlanta, probably not too many. They finished the regular season 60-22, seven games better than LeBron James's Cleveland Cavaliers—and then got swept in the Eastern Conference Finals by the Cavs.

The sole focus of our meetings in Toronto was to probe how we could do better in the postseason. We went through the strengths and weaknesses of every player on the roster. We talked about the kind of players we might want to select in the upcoming NBA draft, or sign as free agents. We went through our coaching philosophy—what worked, what didn't, what we might change.

There were no answers, exactly, for how we had gotten swept by a team that was no better than us—and certainly no excuses. There were some explanations worth talking about.

Kyle Lowry, our point guard and the emotional heart and soul of the team, had played way too many minutes during the regular season. DeMar DeRozan, our leading scorer, missed twenty-some games with an injury at midseason. We played really well without him, but guys were tired, especially Kyle, who had to play more minutes than usual. He kept us afloat, but it took a toll.

At an even six feet tall and 196 pounds, Kyle is a bulldog, but he's small by NBA standards, and by the time the playoffs rolled around that year, I think he was out of gas. That was one of our biggest problems.*

After the season I definitely felt like my job was on the line, that we might all get fired. Getting swept by a team we could have beaten—in the year after it seemed like we had taken a big step forward—was about as bad as it gets.

And some guys did lose their jobs. I survived and so did Dwane Casey, but for about a month I was the only assistant coach left.

I think what saved me is that the offensive schemes I helped introduce had clearly paid off. Like all sports, the NBA has become more focused on metrics and more interested in what you might call the numbers behind the numbers.

To give one example, for many years, the league looked mostly at shooting percentage: how many shots you attempted, how many you made. We now look more closely at "true shooting percentage"—a combination of a player's three-point, two-point, and foul shot attempts. The three-pointer is weighted differently because it comes with an extra point.

The year before I came on staff as an assistant coach, the

---

* Our discussions over this were a kind of prelude to how we handled Kawhi Leonard in our championship season three seasons later—the regular rest periods that became known as "load management."

Raptors were sixteenth in the league in true shooting percentage, about right in the middle. My first season, we improved a little to twelfth—and in that 2013–14 season, we came all the way up to sixth. (Not surprisingly, the Golden State Warriors led the NBA in true shooting during their run of championships and appearances in the Finals.)

The statistics were the result of a simple formula: we were getting better shots and shooting them with better form.

We just needed, somehow, to figure out how to keep doing that once the regular season ended and we reached the part of the year that counts most.

We finally figured out how to advance in the playoffs, but in each of the next three seasons we were stopped by the same roadblock: LeBron James.

In 2016, we won two playoff series, over the Indiana Pacers and Miami Heat, with each of them going the full seven games. Those victories were a big deal—in the Raptors' twenty-year history to that point, the franchise had only succeeded in winning one previous playoff series, and that was back in 2001.

Kyle had a monster game in the clincher against the Heat, with thirty-five points, including five of his seven three-point attempts. That brought us to the Cavaliers. It looked good for a while. We split the first four games, but then lost the final two—and they weren't close. We went down by a combined fifty-four points. LeBron did what LeBron does: he scored, rebounded, passed to teammates for open shots, totally controlled the action.

It got worse in the next two seasons. In each of them, we won our first-round series—over the Milwaukee Bucks and

Washington Wizards—and then were swept in the conference semifinals by the Cavaliers. Eight games, eight losses.

The 2017 series included only one close game, the last one. But the next series, in the spring of 2018, was the killer for us. We had a hell of a regular season, 59-23, the best record in the East and nine games better than the Cavaliers. That gave us the home court advantage, with the first two games in Toronto.

You shouldn't be able to lose a best-of-seven series in the first game, but sometimes it goes in such a way that it can really take the air out of a team. We jumped all over the Cavs at the start and led 33–19 at the end of the first quarter.

We kept the lead for the entire game—and by that, I mean forty-seven minutes and thirty seconds of the forty-eight minutes of regulation play—until LeBron hit a jump shot with thirty seconds left in the fourth quarter. OG Anunoby was guarding him, without any double-team help. He did as good a job as anyone can do. LeBron backed him down to about twelve feet from the hoop, lowered his butt, and faded away as he shot. That's an unguardable shot. It either goes in or it doesn't, and LeBron swished it. That tied the score at 105.

Up to that moment, we had caught LeBron on an off night. For the game, he would finish one for eight on his three-point attempts and just one for six on his free throws. But he hit that shot when his team needed it most. (And an "off night" for LeBron is relative. He still finished with a triple-double—twenty-six points, thirteen rebounds, and eleven assists.)

The end of regulation was excruciating. Kyle Lowry, just as we designed it, drove the ball along the baseline. He did not have a decent shot himself and threw a beautiful pass to a wide-open Fred VanVleet at the top of the arc. Fred missed but DeMar DeRozan was able to grab the offensive rebound cleanly and put a shot back up that spun out. After that we got three point-blank attempts at tip-ins—*three*—and none of them went down.

We did not crumble in overtime—we stayed right with them and had another shot at the buzzer to win it—but ended up losing, 113–112. It was only Game 1 but it was a really tough deal to recover from, emotionally.

We lost another tight one before the series was over—105–103 in Cleveland—on a jump shot by LeBron with no time left on the clock. It came right after we had tied it up on a three-pointer by OG Anunoby with eight seconds left—an incredible shot considering the pressure involved. We had played from behind most of the night and charged back, but it didn't matter.

I think we were spent by Game 4. Nothing left at all. We got blown out of the building, 128–93.

Counting the two defeats at the end of that 2015 series, we lost ten straight postseason games to the Cavaliers. I don't know what the record for consecutive playoff losses to one franchise is, but I'm thinking we could have it.

Our team included the core of players who would help us win an NBA title the following season—including Kyle Lowry, OG Anunoby, Serge Ibaka, Pascal Siakam, Fred VanVleet, Norman Powell. We didn't have Marc Gasol yet—and I don't think anyone was even dreaming that we'd end up with Kawhi Leonard on our roster.

You always learn through defeat and we definitely carried lessons forward from the losses to Cleveland. For our young guys, especially, they just had to go through it. It was their NBA growing pains on the way to a championship.

Three days after we were knocked out of the playoffs, Dwane Casey was named Coach of the Year in a vote by the league's thirty head coaches. It was based solely on the regular season, and well deserved, because it had been a great year.

But the NBA, like all professional sports, is an unforgiving environment. Two days after receiving that honor, Dwane was fired. He couldn't survive a second straight sweep by the Cavs.

I was interviewed a couple of times for the job, and they talked to other people, too. The whole six weeks it was open, I was getting all these texts from people I knew. *What's going on? Why are they taking so long? When do you think you'll hear something?*

I was the least nervous person in my whole circle of family and friends. My years of coaching overseas—dealing with the whims of management and financial downturns and all that—had conditioned me to rolling with whatever came my way. So, too, had getting that first offer to be an assistant coach with the Raptors and then seeing it vanish when Bryan Colangelo got fired. If there was ever a time in my life that I believed things just fell into place, I was well past it.

A couple of other factors gave me some peace of mind. One was that people around the league—front office executives and the personnel within teams' data analytics departments—paid close attention to what other teams were doing.

When they crunched their numbers, our offense looked good. It had grown more efficient year by year, and there were head coaches, general managers, and others who knew I had a lot to do with those improvements. It gave me confidence that I would probably have a job if I needed one. (A story in the *New York Times* described me as the Raptors "offensive coordinator," a term used more in football than basketball.) It might not be as a head coach right away, but I'd land on somebody's staff.

Even the worst-case scenario—that nobody hired me right away—wasn't that bad. The Raptors still owed me for the last year on my assistant coach's deal, so if I had been let go, I would have not worked and got paid for a year. There are worse hardships in life. I still had a fresh memory of coming home from England broke, so having that year left on my deal was a relief.

⌃

When I finally got the call, both Masai Ujiri and Bobby Webster, the team's top executives, were on the line. Masai said, "We're talking to the new coach of the Toronto Raptors."

They had talked to my agent, but I did not have the status for there to be any big negotiation. After I got the phone call, I headed to the team offices to sign my new contract.

I rode along Toronto's downtown streets on my bicycle, a retro black-and-white beach cruiser with no gears, so I could not have raced over there even if I wanted to. It was a short ride, less than ten minutes, through a neighborhood known as Liberty Village. I locked up the bike in the parking garage, walked up a flight of stairs to the team president's office, and put my signature on a three-year contract.

I would be the ninth man to hold that title since the franchise started in 1995. Dwane had held it the longest—seven years.

I was only fifty years old. But if you counted the year I spent after graduation at Northern Iowa as a student assistant, my first year leading an NBA team would be my thirtieth season as a basketball coach.

⌃

9

FLATHEAD LAKE, MONTANA

SPITTING OUT CHERRY PITS WITH PHIL JACKSON

The 1996 Birmingham Bullets. Birmingham is where I won

my first title since the high school championship in Iowa.

(Nurse family collection)

Phil Jackson referred to his offensive system as "a series of complex, coordinated moves, depending on how the defense responds." He also called it "five-man tai chi."

The offense I helped install as a Raptors assistant, and what I run as head coach, has evolved beyond the triangle that Jackson and Tex Winter made famous. The game has changed, the officiating has changed (you can no longer put your hands on a ball handler on the perimeter), and I've broken up the triangle to create more dribble drives into the lane and kick-out passes to three-point shooters.

I have referred to it as the Monk Offense—a reference to the legendary jazz pianist and composer Thelonious Monk. (In truth, I borrowed the term. I first heard it from veteran coach and offensive innovator Ron Ekker.)

Great jazz has a structure beneath it and the artists are deeply grounded in its fundamentals. But there's also a freedom and spontaneity. The musicians step forward and create, and the great ones innovate. That's how I see basketball. Free-flowing and seemingly random—but with everyone versed in the underlying system. It only works if we're all speaking the same language.

This is a good place to write a little about my relationship to music. If you walk into my office, you see the connections right away. On the walls are pictures of Monk, Muddy Waters, BB King, and Chet Baker.

When I was little, my mother made me take piano lessons. Her side of the family was musically talented, and some of them had studied music and taught it. But like a lot of children put into music instruction—and probably like 90 percent of the ones obsessed with sports who wanted to be outside all the time—I absolutely hated it.

I took my lessons from a nun who taught at our school. I think the only time I ever really played was when she was trying to teach me, which went on from about fourth through sixth grade before I was allowed to quit.

I did learn to read music, at least minimally, and in high school I started playing around with music again, on my own. I'd try to play "Purple Rain," or whatever else I might be listening to, and it would take me at least three months to get it to where it sounded a little like something that a person listening to it might recognize as the same song.

Years later, when I got back from England, and in the months before I started coaching the Iowa Energy, I figured I had some time on my hands, so I should do a little self-improvement. I started taking classes at the Harvard Extension School, and one that I signed up for was called the History of the Blues in America. It was taught by a professor named Charlie Sawyer, who had traveled with BB King and written a biography of him.

The class went up online on a Tuesday night, and I'd sometimes participate live if I could, or I'd get up first thing Wednesday morning and link in. I looked forward to it because it was basically a two-hour jam session. He brought in artists and they would play a little—and then it would go back and forth between their jamming and Charlie interviewing them.

If you wanted an A in the class you needed to do some kind of final project, and I asked, "What if I learn to play some blues on the piano and at the end of the semester, I'll send in a three-minute cut of what I've got?"

That got approved and I bought a cool piano in Des Moines that I found on Craigslist for $900. I got a teacher who supposedly specialized in the blues, though he wasn't great. I was trying to read notes and I felt like a fourth grader again. It was hard, but I was working my ass off at it because I had this project I needed to complete.

Charlie and I struck up a friendship. Toward the end of the semester I told Charlie I wanted to attend one of the on-campus classes in Cambridge, and he suggested I come to the last one, which was a big jam session with four bands at the student union building. While I was there, I told him I wanted to continue learning the piano, and he set me up with David Maxwell, who has since passed away but was one of the great blues pianists of all time. He played with Bonnie Raitt, John Lee Hooker, Muddy Waters, and many others.

I got a lesson from Maxwell in Boston. He would play something and show me what he was doing with his hands, and then I'd try to do it. I couldn't really replicate the sounds he was making, but it was one of the great learning experiences of my life, and it got me excited about what was possible if I threw myself into it.

When I was in school, all the way through college, I was never as good a student as I could have been. I was clever enough to get decent grades without a full effort, but I never really invested in learning for learning's sake. I was one of those people for whom the saying "education is wasted on the young" definitely applied, but I've tried to make up for it ever since.

I have a piano that I play in my Raptors office. When the team is on the road, I travel with a portable keyboard and always find time to play. My ability level is probably around the equivalent of having a 12 handicap in golf; I'm far from a professional, but not bad for an amateur.

It's calming for me, almost like meditation. I don't think about basketball when I'm playing music, but I'm pretty sure it helps free the creative part of my brain.

And it also helps give me another frame for thinking about what I face during the season with the unpredictability of trades and injuries. With new guys coming in with some regularity, and other players having to shift positions, it's helpful to think of myself as leading a permanent jam session. Just have to make sure everybody who sits in knows the tunes, and as the band leader, I do what I can to get them comfortable.

My reaction to getting named head coach of the Raptors was not that I had earned it because I was super smart and knew everything it would take to succeed, but that I better hurry up and learn more. That's my mode—stave off whatever anxiety or insecurity I might have by trying to cram in more knowledge and wisdom.

I set off on a little tour of America, stopping in on old mentors as well as some coaches whom I respected but had never met. One of my destinations was Traverse City, Michigan, to see Eldon Miller, my coach at Northern Iowa. (He came in to replace my first coach there, the one who decided in the middle of the season that he'd had enough.)

Coach is still sharp, but he does not hear well, especially in his right ear. He picked me up at the airport and we drove to his place, which was about forty-five minutes away. I was on his right side, in the passenger seat, so it was not easy to communicate.

About halfway there, he turns to me and says, in a very loud voice, "You want to know what it's all about?"

That was his opening statement, since before that there was no conversation going on. I said, "Sure, Coach, I definitely want to know. What's it about?"

And he said, even louder this time, "Playing to win without fear! That's what it's all about. Playing without fear!"

That resonated with me right away because it fit our situation in Toronto. We played fearless, confident basketball during the season—three straight seasons with more than fifty wins—and then as soon as the playoffs started, we lost our swagger. We played with fear, and every time we caught a bad break or lost a close game, it got worse.

When fans look at players, I think they tend to focus on what looks like their immense power and confidence. It's understandable. They're built like Greek gods and they're famous and rich. You figure they have the world by the tail and imagine that if you were in their place, you'd never have a bad day.

But a lot of players have fears. They fear losing. They fear not living up to their contracts. They fear playing poorly and letting the team down. They do not want to be the one with the ball in their hands at the end of a game because someone else is a better shooter. Well, guess what? If you end up with the ball and it's a shot you can make, you've got to let it fly. If you don't, you're strangling the whole team with your anxiety. You're spreading it.

As a coach, you can't deny those fears exist. Players put themselves in boxes because of fear and limit their own possibilities. This became something we talked about from training camp on, and I made it into an acronym—FEAR, which stood for Face Everything And Rise. It was a way of saying that we acknowledge our fears but we're going to look at them head-on and defeat them.

The FEAR slogan sort of fit me and my personality. I had failed at various points in my career, but I don't think it was ever out of some fear I couldn't face. I left home and went off to coach older guys in England. I started a D-League team from scratch in Des Moines. When I moved on to the Rio Grande Valley Vipers, and they asked me to do all this experimental stuff, I wasn't afraid to try it.

That had to be my attitude as I started off coaching my first NBA team—that basically, I'm going for it, man. Every single day. After working so hard to get an opportunity, I couldn't approach it as something I was afraid to lose. I couldn't start playing it safe.

︿

The Raptors director of sports science, Alex McKechnie, is a distinguished-looking man—gray hair, cool black-framed glasses—who goes by the nickname Silver. He is an integral part of everything we do and was the person in the organization responsible for shaping how we would help restore Kawhi Leonard to good health when he came to us in 2018 after being injured almost the entire previous season. (More on that later.)

Alex spent five years with Phil Jackson in Los Angeles. On the day I got the job, he came into my office and said, "I'm going to set you up with Phil." A few days later, he texted us both and said, "You guys sort it out."

At that point, I was just Nick from the D-League and Phil Jackson was the man with thirteen NBA championships—the two he won playing for Red Holzman's legendary New York Knicks teams, the six he won with Michael Jordan and the Bulls, and the five he added on with Shaq, Kobe, and the Lakers.

But other than the small matter of his thirteen rings and Hall of Fame status, we did have a few things in common. We were both Midwesterners who had played college basketball at schools no one much cared about—me at Northern Iowa and Phil about 580 miles north, at the University of North Dakota. And despite the fact that he had a significant playing career in the NBA—a dozen seasons between 1967 and 1980—he had to fight his way into coaching in the league just like I did.

Phil was an assistant coach with the NBA's New York Nets for a couple of years after his playing career, and then between 1982 and 1987, he coached the Albany Patroons of the old Continental Basketball Association. (He jokingly referred to the CBA as the Cockroach Basketball Association.) For four summers, he coached teams in Puerto Rico, in what was known as the Superior Basketball League—a job that he has written taught him valuable lessons in "how to cope with chaos." (The fans were so rowdy that the courts were encircled with wire fencing.)

He could not get a job in the NBA. All of the out-of-the-box thinking he was later celebrated for was considered a little too out there for the people making the hiring decisions.

NBA players back in his day made only a fraction of what they do now, even adjusted for inflation. He would not have emerged from his playing career as a wealthy man. He even considered going to law school at one point and may have made the leap if Bulls general manager Jerry Krause had not offered him an assistant coaching job in 1987.

I can relate to that. At one low point in my time in England, I thought, maybe I'll just pack up and go home. I got as far as making a list of three or four other things I might want to do. Unfortunately, when I looked at the options I put down, they all looked like absolute shit to me.

I suppose that's when I confronted the fact that I was a lifelong coach. A basketball lifer.

And I decided at that moment, just get off your ass, man. Try to compete harder. Fight like hell. Try to learn more. Let's read some more sports psychology books and figure out how to reach these guys another way. Let's study winning. Let's look at more tape of out-of-bounds plays so I can steal a couple more wins somewhere.

I think this current generation thinks sometimes that getting ahead is all about making contacts—write this guy an email, try to bump into this other guy at a camp or in a hotel lobby. And I'm not saying that's not important. If I knew more people, things would have happened faster for me.

But you can't skip the step of working your ass off and learning your craft. If you get the job you're dreaming about, that's great, but do you know how to do it? Did you really get yourself ready, or did all your energy just go into figuring out how to climb the ladder?

⌃

Phil got back to me quickly after Alex put us together and asked me to fly out to talk with him where he lived, in Flathead Lake, Montana. He was in his early seventies and retired, having left his last NBA job, president of the New York Knicks, about a year before.

I flew to Glacier Park International Airport and made my way to a motel I had reserved in Flathead Lake without knowing how long Phil wanted to give me. An hour, a lunch, a day? I had no idea.

When I called to say I'd landed, he gave me directions to his local coffee shop. I had a semi-formal list of things I wanted to ask him about, but a conversation with him does not go in a straight line. We talked for a couple of hours, just circling around things about his life—him asking me about my life and career, different basketball people we both knew—and then after a while, he said, "Let's go, man."

We jumped in his truck and drove maybe a quarter of a mile before he stopped at this farm stand—it was cherry season there—and he bought this big-ass bag and plopped it down between us and rolled the windows down. And for the next two and a half hours, we proceeded to drive around the lake eating cherries.

And I'm there thinking, here I am, sitting with a guy I've studied for all these years—his coaching moves, time-outs, end-of-game strategies, the triangle—and I'm rolling around with him and spitting cherry pits out the window of his truck.

He finally dropped me back at my rental car and said, "Go shower up or do whatever you've got to do. Dinner's at seven-thirty," and told me where to meet him. We had dinner, then drove back to his place and sat on his deck, in these rocking chairs, until about eleven-thirty, and as I was leaving, he said, "Text me when you're up."

The next morning, I met him at the end of a long gravel road, and he was sitting there in one of those four-wheelers, an all-terrain vehicle, and I jumped in and he drove me out to this other cabin that he owns. It was right on the lake, and we talked on the deck for a couple of hours, grabbed some lunch, and when we came back, he said, "Let's go down to the basement."

He said somebody had just sent him some video of the Bulls championship runs—he hadn't looked at it yet—and we just sat down there for a couple of hours, half watching it and just bull-shitting about basketball, his strategies back then, how the game has changed, where he thinks it's going.

We got through the tapes and he said, "I'll meet you again for dinner at the Italian place." He was incredibly generous with his time. It ended up being a three-day visit, and it was helpful in getting my mind right for what was in front of me.

We didn't talk much about the triangle offense. And besides, it would be a huge waste to get time with Phil and use it to just geek out on nuts-and-bolts basketball.

I'd ask him a question and he would circle the house for an hour before he got to an answer—but everything in between was well worth the time.

As a lot of people know, Phil is spiritual. He grew up in a strict Pentecostal household—his dad was a minister—and as an adult he has been attracted to Eastern faiths and Native American religious practices. (His best-known book is *Sacred Hoops*.) He wrote that the team area of the Bulls' training site was where "the spirit of the team takes form" and was a "holy sanctuary. The place where the players and the coaches come together and prepare our hearts and minds for battle."

In the time I spent with him in Montana, Phil, true to form, often mixed earthly basketball wisdom with something akin to spiritual guidance. What I took as his message was that lots of stuff was in my control as a coach, but that if I did not handle things correctly, heavenly forces would make sure I paid a price.

He cautioned me that I always had to put the needs of the group first—before myself or any individual. "First and foremost, don't underestimate the basketball gods," he said as we sat out on his deck one of those evenings. "What do I mean by that? Here's what I mean. You've been hired to make every decision that's best for the team. If you don't do that, you're going to run into some godly problems."

Another thing that he left me with was his advice on my interactions with players. There were times I'd need to be tough and raise my voice—and others when I'd have to be more like a gentle parent.

"I want you to imagine you got a sword in your hand," he said. "You have one end that's really sharp. You're going to need to use that to prod them and get on their asses and motivate them and push them further. But every now and then, I want you to look at the handle of the sword. And that's going to represent compassion. You're going to have to understand where they've come from and what they're going through at the moment."

All successful coaches know what methods work for them. I couldn't set out to be a copy of Phil Jackson or anyone else. I wanted to pick up what I could to adapt for myself.

Coaching a professional team always entails teaching some complex tactics. A normal fan, or even players at lower levels of basketball, are not going to fully grasp what we try to do on offense or defense. (I've got players who sometimes don't!)

When I visited with Joe Maddon, who was then managing the Chicago Cubs, he stressed the value of communicating a small set of broad principles that you want your team to follow. Those are more important than game tactics. He set out his principles at the beginning of each season—often on slogans that ended up on T-shirts.

"Embrace the Target," was one, meaning understand what it means to be a championship favorite, and therefore, a target of other teams. "Respect 90" meant go all out on the ninety feet between bases. "Try Not to Suck" was self-explanatory.

Big corporations do a version of the same thing. Amazon probably has some of the most complicated engineering challenges of any company in the world, but a single phrase of its CEO and founder, Jeff Bezos, guides everything they do: "The customer is the most important person in the room."

Apple drills into its employees the mantra "Think different."

These corporations deal with stuff a lot more involved than any basketball team ever would, but they still see value in simplifying their missions to as few words as possible.

I also got a chance to visit with Pete Carroll, the football coach, whom I've long admired. I watched his Seattle Seahawks practice, which was the best I've ever witnessed in any sport at any level.

Carroll has written that after he was fired as head coach of the New England Patriots in 2000 (his successor was Bill Belichick), he decided to write down his principles of coaching. What he stood for. How he wanted his teams to play.

He had been a head coach with two NFL franchises at that point and a defensive coordinator with both college and pro teams. In *Win Forever,* he wrote, "I couldn't believe that I had been coaching for the past twenty-six years and had never stated my philosophy, let alone written it down."

Carroll was inspired by John Wooden's famous "pyramid of success."

By the time training camp rolled around in September 2018, I had my own pyramid, which I had made into a slide and showed the players in our first meeting.

On it were some of the specific features of how we wanted to play. *Assisted buckets* was a reminder that we wanted to share the ball on offense. *Shot spectrum* meant take our shots from the high-percentage areas on the floor. *Ball pressure* and *shot contests* were part of how we wanted to play defense.

There were a number of sayings on the pyramid, or platitudes if you want to be critical about it. "Expect to Win" was one of them, borrowed from my time in Birmingham, England. "Attack the Title." "Let It Rip." "Only the Fearless Can Be Great."

None of the stuff I put up there was complicated. None of it was brilliant. But it was concise and clear, and it stated the principles of how we wanted to play—and, more important, the spirit of how we would compete.

10

TORONTO, THIS TIME AS HEAD COACH

LEARNING THAT MY VOICE IS A FINITE RESOURCE

On the sideline alongside rapper and devoted Raptors fan Drake.

(Vaughn Ridley / Getty Images)

I was one month into my new job as head coach of the Toronto Raptors and about to leave Las Vegas, where I had been watching our Summer League team, when I first heard that we might acquire Kawhi Leonard from the San Antonio Spurs. It was at a breakfast meeting at the hotel with Masai Ujiri and Bobby Webster, a routine get-together before we all split for the airport and went our separate ways.

One of them brought up Kawhi and said something like, "Hey, this is a possibility that you should know about." Ninety-five percent of the time when you hear those things, the trades don't happen. I put in my two cents, like I would with any possible deal, and that was it. You just take in the information and wait to see what happens.

I flew to Des Moines and then drove up to Carroll to visit with my mom and other folks from back home. I wanted to do that before we hit training camp and then got into the grind of the long season.

Late the next night, Bobby called me and said, "This may be going down and I wanted to give you a heads-up that by the time you wake up in the morning, the trade may be done."

And that's what happened. I woke up—the trade was complete—and I had to quickly get on a plane and fly to Toronto to meet with Kawhi.

We acquired him along with Danny Green, a dependable veteran guard and three-point threat. In return, we gave up a first-round draft pick along with Jakob Poeltl and, most significant, DeMar DeRozan—who had played for the Raptors for all nine of his NBA seasons and led the team in scoring in each of the last five.

Anytime there's a trade involving star players, it's complicated on numerous levels. The money has to work out within the salary cap, which is why the trades almost always include multiple players. Teams shake up their rosters, their identities, and sometimes their style of play. This one, though, was even more complicated than most.

DeMar had been the face of the Raptors for a long time. He was not happy about the trade and neither were some of his teammates, especially Kyle Lowry, our point guard. Kyle and DeMar had been teammates on the Raptors for six years, had been through a lot together, and were best friends.

People on the outside tend to think, *Oh, it's just a business,* when players get traded, but that's not always the case. Players have lives, homes, families, and friendships rooted in where they play, especially if they've been there a long time. DeMar was upset. More significant for us, so was Kyle.

As for the guy we were getting, he was at that point the biggest mystery in the NBA. Kawhi, the fifteenth overall pick in the 2011 draft, had been with the Spurs his whole career. He was a physical marvel—six foot seven with a seven-foot-three wingspan and huge, eleven-inch hands—who was initially regarded as primarily a defensive specialist.

But he steadily improved his ballhandling, shooting, and other offensive skills, and by his sixth year in the league, Kawhi was a twenty-five-point-a-game scorer and one of the top five players in the NBA. When the Spurs won the NBA title in 2014, he was named MVP of the Finals.

In the season before he came to us, however, he played just

nine games. He had a knee injury that was not one of the common ones, like a meniscus tear or even an ACL. His was harder to diagnose and treat. The Spurs and Kawhi clashed over his medical care, and trust broke down on both sides.

We could not be sure what we were getting. There were still questions about not just Kawhi's physical condition, but also his state of mind. It wasn't clear he was any happier about the trade than DeMar was.

Kawhi was on the last year of his contract and, by most accounts, intent on going back home to Southern California to sign with one of the LA teams—the Clippers or Lakers—as soon as he could. The word was that he would have preferred to have been dealt to either of them—to jump-start that process by a year—rather than go north of the border to Toronto.

The trade was high risk, high reward. There was certainly going to have to be a lot of work done to help put him back together. All the stories after the trade said that the Raptors had taken a big chance by dealing a healthy franchise mainstay for a possibly injured and unhappy star. As one put it, we had "rolled the dice," and it was hard to disagree with that assessment.

But I think the way I'd say it is that management had seen enough playoff failure and was ready for a gamble. Sure, we had experienced some good moments in the playoffs over the past several seasons, but they were outweighed by the disappointments.

There was the sweep by Washington. The sweep by the Cavs in 2017. And then the sweep in 2018 just sealed it—because the Cavs had not had a good year at all and were as vulnerable as they had been in any recent season. And we were really good.

We had won fifty-nine games in the 2017–18 regular season.

You just don't tear a team like that up without giving it a lot of thought. But the front office had finally seen enough and decided to shake things up, which I totally understood and supported. In their own way, they were playing without fear.

⌃

Kawhi had a reputation for being extremely quiet, to the point of being someone who just doesn't talk. He was also known for having a sharp basketball mind.

I met with him at first in the boardroom at our practice site along with our front office guys. They talked and he mostly didn't. I couldn't tell if he was in shock to have ended up with us—or just pissed.

After a while, everyone else cleared out and left me alone with him. I figured, okay, I'm the new coach here, he doesn't know that much about me, so let me go into a little spiel about who I am and where I came from. I told him about my background—England, some of the stuff I did in the D-League, my five seasons as a Raptors assistant—and then we started looking forward.

I said, here's who you're probably going to be in the starting lineup with, here's some of the other rotation guys, and here's how I build my offense. I was up at the whiteboard (my comfort zone) drawing stuff, and the next thing I know, he's out of his seat, he's got a marker in his hand, and he's up there with me and putting stuff on the board.

He said he likes certain things I've drawn but he has some of his own ideas. For example, on a particular pin-down screen, there was an option that maybe I was not seeing, and he showed me and said we can try that. He liked what I've put up there about our transition attack but saw another option there, too.

I was thinking: I can see what people meant. This guy is tuned in and smart as hell. And I was not surprised, by the way.

Players in the NBA's elite tier are in almost all cases among the league's most intelligent players. They marry their extraordinary physical gifts to their intellects. On top of that, they have a work ethic that goes beyond what the average player is willing to endure. That's how you get a superstar.

I've written that it's hard to stand up in front of a group of NBA players for the first time. You're not being paranoid if you think they're judging you—they really are.

The Xs and Os are probably 15 percent of coaching, but it's what matters initially to the players. They want to see that you can put them in positions on the court to succeed—build on their strengths, hide their weaknesses, increase their value.

I went through the same thing in the D-League. A lot of those players came from the big-time NCAA programs and played for coaches who were a hundred times more famous than I am. They might have been stuck in Des Moines or the Rio Grande Valley, but they still had a big sense of themselves.

The question when you get up in front of these guys is always the same: Who the fuck are you? Until you lay the plan out for them—this is how we're going to play; this is how you fit in and how you'll benefit—they have zero trust in you.

I'm sure that's a lot of what was going on between Kawhi and me, although he is a different kind of cat—self-contained, confident, and genuinely not interested in personal statistics or acclaim. After he signed a $94 million contract in San Antonio, someone wrote about the car he was still driving, a twenty-year-old Chevy Tahoe he had bought used back when he was in high school. The writer ran the make and model through an online database and calculated that it was worth $1,390—or maybe a little more if he had added some options.

That day when we first talked in Toronto, Kawhi stopped it after about thirty-five minutes. He looked me in the eye and said, "I'll give you a year. I don't know what's going to happen after that, but I'm going to play my ass off, and we'll play to win it all."

I appreciated his directness. Like me, he was someone who liked to address the elephant in the room.

Before the start of the 2018–19 season, I had a couple thousand rubber bracelets made with the letters AMJ on them—which stood for April, May, June. The message was that it would be those months, when the playoffs take place, that count for us. The letters represented what we would build toward from the very first day of training camp.

I gave the bracelets to the players and some (not all) wore them. I walked around the arena and gave them to ushers, security people, whoever I ran into. I still have people who stop me in Toronto to show me they're still wearing the bracelets.

It was like the trick I had pulled out of my bag in Birmingham, a quarter century before, when I plastered the slogan "Expect to Win" everywhere to counter that franchise's longtime losing culture.

The Raptors did not have a losing culture. In fact, we had piled up a ton of regular season victories over the previous three seasons as well as a regular-season Eastern Conference championship, and it had been six years since we had a losing record.

But we were severe underperformers in the postseason. The bracelet had two messages on it. One was AMJ and the other was EXPECT TO WIN.

Getting Kawhi was not one of those trades that made us an instant favorite to win the NBA title. It was nothing like that. He was not regarded in the same way as a LeBron, or a Michael Jordan in his prime. Just having him on your team didn't automatically send you to the top of the heap.

When healthy, he was a legitimate star and highly respected, but on the terrific Spurs teams he played for he was part of an ensemble with Tim Duncan, Tony Parker, and Manu Ginóbili. In the championship they won together, in 2014, he was still just twenty-two, and the team's third-leading scorer.

In the preseason, when we were mentioned among the teams that could compete for the title, we were well down the list of contenders—behind the Warriors, Celtics, Rockets, Lakers, and sometimes the 76ers.

When the games started, we were still dealing some with the emotional fallout from the trade. Kyle Lowry and I had been close in the years I was an assistant coach. I was helping run the offense and he was the point guard, so we had a lot of conversations, but not all of them were even about basketball.

But he wasn't talking to me much that fall, or to anyone else, really. Fortunately, whatever was going on internally did not turn out to matter on the court. We got off to a blazing start, with wins in twelve of our first thirteen games, and most of them were not close. Our average margin of victory was almost eleven points.

A lot of that had to do with Kyle. He always comes out of the gate firing away, in great shape, and fresh. He's an early guy at the training site. If we have a practice on an off day or a shootaround on the morning of a game, he'll arrive at eight, get his shots up and his massage or other treatments in, and by the time the rest of the team rolls in he's already been in there for a couple of hours.

I remember reading a book by Alex Ferguson, the longtime manager of Manchester United, where he wrote about all the magical skills that David Beckham seemed to possess. He said the one thing he wished fans understood was how hard Beckham worked—that even after he reached the top, he was practicing all that stuff religiously. The rest of the team would be headed for the locker room after a training session and Beckham would be out on the pitch by himself, bending corner kicks toward the goal.

It's the same in the NBA. The best players never stop trying to add skills and get better. I don't want to make it sound like they're going down into a coal mine every day, but most people would not imagine the work that players like Kyle put in—both during the season and in the summers.[*]

The fringe players at the edge of NBA rosters, or trying to get onto one, are under constant evaluation. They're playing

---

[*] Marc Gasol is another example. He played all through the summer of 2019 with the Spanish national team. When he got to training camp, we held him out of team practices in order to rest him, and it was killing him. He's thirty-four years old and has played a dozen years in the league, but if you came into the gym, you would have seen him off to the side for hours at a time, working on individual skills while the rest of the team was practicing.

on Summer League teams, working out in informal preseason training camps. It's an all-year grind.

~

I was pretty calm as the season started, even in our first game — and not overly emotional. Sure, in some ways, it felt like it had been a long time coming. But I did not have an adjustment to make to the style of play in the NBA (as I did in some of my previous jobs), because I had been on the sideline as an assistant for five seasons.

And being the head coach was totally comfortable. It's what I had been most of my career.

In our opening game victory, which was at home over Cleveland, Kyle scored twenty-seven points on ten-of-twelve shooting, including five out of his six three-pointers. He kept it up those first few weeks—Kawhi, too, was playing really well—and everyone else followed along.

We were extremely careful with Kawhi from the beginning all the way through the end of the season. When we had games on back-to-back nights, he didn't play them both. We limited his minutes per game and were careful not to play him for long stretches, nothing beyond ten minutes.

But when he was out there playing, he looked like peak Kawhi— as good as or better than he had been in San Antonio. I had a meeting with him a few weeks in, just to check in on how he was feeling. He told me everything was good. When I asked what he thought of the systems we were running, he said, "The offense is cool. The defense, I don't know, I think it needs some tweaks."

And he was right about that. I was saving some coverages for the postseason. From there, I said I wanted to talk about whatever personal goals he had—that I had seen enough in ten games or whatever it was to think he could win an MVP award. "I don't have any interest in that," he said. "All I want is to be healthy. I want to play a long time. I want to play for championships. That's all I care about."

In mid-November, we hit a little skid and lost three straight games—the first two at home to the New Orleans Pelicans and Detroit Pistons, neither of which were considered elite teams, and the third in Boston to the Celtics, one of our main rivals in the East.

I remember being in the film room the next day. It was a little edgy. It's pro sports, and the day-to-day pressure is real.

We were all talking about some specific game clips up on the screen, and a conversation broke out about how we need more ball movement. It gained some energy on one side of the room. Some of the second-unit guys were saying things like, "Yeah, we moved the ball last year, we really popped it around. And they couldn't stop us."

Somebody said something about swinging the ball around early in the shot clock, just so more people get touches and we get back in the mindset that we're a passing team. And that got a murmur of approval.

Suddenly, Kawhi said, loudly, "Yo!"

And I said, "Yes, Kawhi?"

He said, "I ain't passing the ball for the fucking hell of it. My job is to score or to draw multiple defenders, and when I kick it out to you, then it's your job to score."

That was a moment for all of us. In the huddle, in the locker room, in the film room, Kawhi was always locked in. I'm not sure I've had a more attentive player anywhere. Maybe a walk-on at one of my college jobs.

But he had not said a whole lot. When he did that day, it was like: Boom! The quiet man has spoken. There's always an added impact when that happens. The words count more.

And he was right, of course. We do want to pass the ball, and we actually count our passes each game. It's one of the many data points our analytics staff track. Usually, the more passes the better. But each pass has to have a purpose—and that didn't seem to be what was being proposed.

That meeting was a moment of growth, a turning point. Up until then, I think there was a little bit of doubt about Kawhi, or an inability to read him—sort of, who is this guy? Why are there some nights he rests and doesn't play?

I understood it. The way we were handling him was new and an adjustment for everyone.

But after he spoke up, I think everyone got the point, in case there had been any doubts, that he was not a guy just putting in time until he got to his next stop. He was going to help lead us, in his own way.

Darrell Mudra wrote that the strength of a leader "is determined by the effectiveness and the growth of his subordinates...As his leadership improves, he becomes less and less necessary."

I wouldn't want to take that to its extreme and delegate myself right out of a job, but when I became the head coach, I decided I was going to have less, not more, to say to my team. This applied specifically to the eighty-two-game regular season rather than the playoffs.

Another hero of mine, Thelonious Monk, once said that nothing is as powerful as silence. It may seem like an odd thing coming from a man who made some of the most beautiful music in history, but what he meant, I'm pretty sure, was the silence between the notes—the pauses when a listener anticipates, even just for a moment, what's coming next.

The jazz critic Peter Watrous once wrote that with Monk, "everything is between the cracks, a bit faster or slower than the obvious would suggest, and without his tempos the compositions don't work as well."

I would never compare myself to a genius like Monk, but coaching has a tempo and a rhythm, too. I believed that if I held back a little from October until we reached the postseason in mid-April—if I allowed for some quiet, and even some silences—my words would carry more power when they mattered the most.

If you walked into one of our practices and didn't know what I looked like, there's a good chance you wouldn't pick me out as the head coach. First of all, there are a lot of people out there in addition to the players—all the coaches, plus some of the data analytics and video people. (If they're former players, and many are, they're on the floor helping players with their individual work.)

At practices, I'm usually stationed at a corner of the court, often alone. I'm normally wearing jeans, a sweatshirt, my black baseball cap with the bill pulled down low. Nothing is happening out there that I have not meticulously planned in meetings with my assistants, but they're the ones running the show.

I'll have a couple of things to say when the players and coaches all gather at the center circle at the beginning of practice—and then again when we return to the circle at the end. Other than that, you might hear my voice two or three times over the course of ninety minutes and there's a good chance it's to say something positive.

My interactions with players only rarely take place in sit-down meetings. They're young guys. Athletes. They don't want to sit down. If you can get them to take their earbuds out, that qualifies as a formal get-together.

I'll grab one of them for a couple of minutes before practice or after practice and we'll have extended conversations—except that they occur in snippets.

At one point I was stressing that I wanted whoever grabbed a rebound to push the ball themselves on the dribble and lead a fast break if they had the opportunity. OG Anunoby complained to me after one practice that Fred VanVleet kept coming back to him and demanding the ball. That's what point guards have traditionally done: look for an outlet pass and take control of the ball. I'm sure it's what Fred had been trained to do since he started playing basketball.

I saw OG the next day in a hotel corridor, as I was walking to my room. "He's still doing it," he said, without stopping.

I filed that away. It was part of one of those ongoing conversations.

I try to have a praise-to-criticism ratio of six to one. I don't chart it, but it's a goal and I probably get close enough to achieving it. It's not how I was coached back in the day, but I think it's a good guideline for anybody running anything—a team, a business, a family.

I'll be out there clapping my hands and saying, "great pass," "great ball pressure," "way to block out"—just reinforcing the components of what adds up to winning basketball. That kind of praise costs me nothing, and it builds goodwill and positive relationships.

I'll also use humor with players—as much as I can and sometimes even in the middle of the game. If you're laughing, you're loose. If everybody's grim all the time, it's a long march to eighty-two games.

We had one game where Norman Powell was struggling to make shots, but we had injuries and a really short bench. I said to him as we were going into the fourth quarter, "You want to know the good news and the bad news, Norm?"

He looked at me, waiting for what was coming next. "You're two for ten, but I can't take you out because there's nobody else sitting over there."

A lot of fans probably do not realize it, but at our practices—and I'm pretty sure at the practices of every NBA team—the scoreboard and clock are always on. They're on if we're going five-on-five full court, if we're going three-on-three half court, or if we've got just two guys out there in an end-of-the-game drill. Put ten seconds on the clock, put the ball in one player's hands, and let him go at the defender. Can he score and win the game, or does the other guy stop him?

The rest of the team is circled around, watching, rooting, talking trash. Believe me, those two guys go at it.

During the heart of the season, we don't have that much opportunity for full practices, but when we do, we're focused. I often put ninety seconds up on the clock, or a minute—the end-of-game situations that I learned in Iowa get everybody locked in and concentrating.

Anybody can run practice with guys just running up and down the court. You do some drills, they break a sweat, and everybody feels good. I think some AAU practices look like that, probably a lot of high school practices.

You can get a little bit out of that. A coach observes and when he sees something he doesn't like, blows the whistle and steps in and corrects. But I want to put players in stressful situations. That's how you get better as a team.

We keep score in practices because it's how professional players are wired. They're competitive as hell. That and their talent is what got them to the NBA. If they lose in a drill, they're pissed. If they think a teammate fouled them and you didn't call it, they scream about it. This could be in training camp as they're fighting for playing time, at an off-day practice in the middle of the long slog of a road trip, or on some random morning in Sacramento. It doesn't matter.

People sometimes wonder if it's harder to coach in the NBA. My short answer: "Are you kidding me?"

The NBA is easier, by far, because the resources available to us are overwhelming. Nothing is spared. If a player can't practice, you might see him in a corner of the gym, on a massage table, getting treatment from one of our staff of therapists. We have nutritionists. Sports psychologists. Athletic trainers and assistant trainers.

There are cameras everywhere at our training site and they have facial recognition technology. It's called the NoahFace System. If a player is in the gym shooting—during practice, before or after, or if he comes in late at night to get shots up, which some of them do—the software logs every shot.

Good shooters want to swish the ball in practice—make it without hitting iron. That's perfection, and it takes any element of luck out of the equation. I learned that from Des Flood (Dr. Shot) back in Iowa. He would say, "How hard can you concentrate when you're practicing to swish it, because if you make that your benchmark, you're increasing your margin of error."

In our gym, when you start shooting, the cameras track everything—your arc, your depth, if you were wide right, wide left. We love that because we can say to them, "Hey, you took a hundred free throws when you were in the gym last night at midnight and you only had fifty-eight of them go straight within our guidelines. So let's work on it."

In the championship season, Kyle went on a little cold streak and we figured, let's pull all the data and see if anything jumps out at us. It did. His arc had dropped to 41 degrees. When he's shooting well and the ball's going in, it's usually at 46 or 47 degrees. So he knew that's what he had to correct. He did—and he was right back in sync.

We always have music at our practices, which I started doing in England (I got the idea from reading Pete Carroll's book) and really stepped up in the Rio Grande Valley. We started doing what we called "speed practices," where we picked twelve songs and twelve drills, each of them three minutes long. When the song switched, the drill switched, and we just flew from one thing to the next.

In Toronto, we have a DJ at every practice. As far as I know, we're the only NBA team with a DJ. I tell him to pump the music up. It's fun. It livens things up.

If we're scrimmaging and one of my assistants is trying to communicate with his squad, sometimes they get mad at me. The music's too loud and the players can't hear them. I say to them, "Welcome to my world."

It's kind of a joke, but the seriousness behind it is that practices should simulate games in every way possible—including the noise level inside an NBA arena. I tell them to get used to it; that's what it's going to be like if you ever get to do it for real.

I think my coaching staff reflects the makeup of the league, in all the best ways. It includes Adrian Griffin, who played nine seasons in the NBA for five different teams, and Jim Sann, who has been a scout, video coordinator, or assistant coach with four different franchises. Players will not encounter much in the course of a season that those two have not seen before.

I have Nate Bjorkgren by my side, whom I have a history with going all the way back to South Dakota and Iowa. In this most recent off-season, I brought Brittni Donaldson onto the staff as an assistant. She is a former point guard at my alma mater, Northern Iowa, though I did not know her until she joined the Raptors data analytics team in 2017. She became the NBA's tenth female assistant, and at twenty-six, its youngest.

Three of our assistants have backgrounds from outside the US. Just as there's a pipeline for international players, there's one for coaches from overseas. In recent years there have been NBA assistant coaches from, among other nations, Argentina, Brazil, Croatia, Greece, and Lithuania.

It just makes sense. As the talent overseas has increased, so has the level of coaching. One of our assistants, Jon Goodwillie, is Canadian, went to college in Canada, and came up through our video department. He was head coach of our Summer League team in Las Vegas in 2019.

Sergio Scariolo has coached pro clubs in Italy, Spain, and Russia, and he was head coach of the Spanish national team that won the 2019 FIBA World Cup in China. (I was the coach of Canada's team, which did not do nearly as well.) Patrick Mutombo was born in Zaire, grew up in the Congo, and played professionally in Italy, Brazil, and Greece.

I think I'd feel at a disadvantage without an international representation on my staff. They keep an eye on their part of the world—on players, new ideas, new ways of doing things. Everything is interconnected now. We're not just exporting basketball players and introducing the game overseas—we're learning from the rest of the world.

The most obvious thing that fans see is the "Euro-step," an offensive move popularized by Manu Ginóbili that is now part of nearly every player's arsenal. (Giannis Antetokounmpo uses it to devastating effect.) At the FIBA tournament, several teams were running elements of our Toronto offense, and I'm not sure I saw any that were not using one of our sideline out-of-bounds plays. (The play was designed by Sergio, so it had some international DNA to start with.)

There have been international players in the NBA since the beginning of the league in the mid-1940s, but the really big influx began in the early 1990s, after NBA players started competing in the Olympics. That brought the NBA to the rest of the world and globalized the sport.

More European players started coming over, and some were high draft picks. Either out of unfamiliarity or a little jealousy, the thinking developed that they were not as tough as American players. That seems ridiculous now, and the reverse may even be true. Some of the international guys I've had—Greivis Vásquez, Serge Ibaka, and many others—are among the most hard-nosed players I've coached.

In general, the international players get thrown to the wolves early. At sixteen years old, they're playing against pros—rather than dominating on the AAU circuit and figuring out which college coaches to let into their living rooms.

Like many other teams in the league, our roster is a little

United Nations. We've got Serge Ibaka, whose early life was split between the Congo and France, Marc Gasol (Spain), Pascal Siakam (Cameroon), Chris Boucher (St. Lucia and Canada), and Oshae Brissett (Canada).

⌃

I told myself when I first got the job that I would have six bullets to fire during the season, just six times that I would allow myself—in the midst of a lackluster practice, after a particularly sloppy game, or during a losing streak—to really rip into the team.

There's a cliché about a coach "losing" his team—or "losing the locker room," as it's sometimes said. It's a real thing. It can happen if you just chew on their asses from day one and never let up. At a certain point, players will feel like they've heard enough and just stop listening.

I don't know for sure that's what happened to me when I was coaching at Grand View, when I was still in my early twenties, but it's always in the back of my mind. Those poor kids had to put up with a coach who yelled too much—who had no concept of the tempo and rhythms required and the uses of silence.

I didn't keep close track of my six bullets (I certainly remember one during the playoffs, which I'll get into a bit later) but I'm fairly sure that I never used them all. There was one other determination I made before the season about how I was going to handle my role. I decided I was not going to run any of the sessions where we looked at game tape.

I put an assistant coach in charge of the offense, another in charge of the defense, and a third in charge of special teams—meaning out-of-bounds plays, late-game plays, any other special situations. I rotated them every eight games to keep them objective. I didn't want the offensive guy to be lobbying for someone who couldn't guard anybody to get minutes, or the other way around.

The players had heard my voice a lot over the last five seasons, because I ran a lot of these meetings. I would eventually step forward and do the critiques—but not until the playoffs.

ALONG THE EIGHTY-TWO-GAME ROAD

COACHING ON PARALLEL TRACKS

With Kawhi Leonard, who stayed a year and helped lead us to an NBA title.

(Jesse D. Garrabrant / NBAE via Getty Images)

A lot of what I've covered in the previous chapter reflects some patience on my part. And I suppose confidence, too, though if things had gone another way maybe it would have looked like foolhardiness.

I was in my first NBA head coaching job. It would be natural for me to want to win as many games as I could—and as fast as I could make that happen. Insecurity could drive that thinking. A certain amount of ego could drive it—my wanting to prove I was worthy of the job.

But we had won 263 regular-season games in the past five seasons, an average of fifty-three each year. That's really good in the NBA. We had been a number one seed in the East headed into the playoffs, a two seed, and a three seed. We hadn't finished the job in any of those years.

Management made it clear, by making a change in the head coach position, that they were not satisfied with the status quo. The focus on the postseason is why I handed out those AMJ bracelets—April, May, and June, the months when the games count most.

Of course we played to win every time the referee tossed the ball up for the opening tip, and we did go on to post an excellent regular season record. But right from the start, we were going forward on parallel missions—playing in the present and looking toward the spring.

A lot of that had to do with developing individual players. Teams get better in two ways. One is that they mesh as a group.

They learn one another's moves and habits. They cover for their teammates' weaknesses and play to their strengths. That is what's commonly referred to as "chemistry."

The other way they progress is that individual players improve, and in the NBA, that's possible from the first day of training camp right through the end of the playoffs. We never stop working with them and giving them chances to demonstrate their new skills, even at the risk of failure. You might lose a game, but in the long run, you may get closer to a championship.

I take a great deal of pride in my ability to develop players—to help them improve their fitness level, their ballhandling, their ability to use their off hand, their shooting. And unlike in the D-League, I have a whole lot of help. We have four people with the title of assistant coach, and in addition to that we have video coordinators, data analysts, athletic trainers, physiotherapists, and strength and conditioning coaches. At our practices, the support staff far outnumbers the players.

The commitment to development in Toronto comes from the very top of the organization—from ownership. There's no budget. You just get it done.

In the off-season, some of our players work out with their personal trainers, but we also send coaches to wherever they are. When I was an assistant coach and Jonas Valančiūnas was our center, I'd go over to Lithuania in the off-season. I would work him out if there was time. If he was playing with the national team, I'd just try to let him know I was there. It could be as simple as saying, "Hey, Jonas. Looking good. Way to go. See you in a couple of weeks."

I may also have a little more patience with developing players—and a passion for helping them prove their doubters wrong—because my own professional advancement took some time. None of the players I coach are finished products, not even the guys in their thirties. They're all on their own journey, just as I was.

At one point in Mudra's book, he writes (quoting the German writer and philosopher Goethe), "If you treat a man as he would and could be, he will become what he would and could be. If you treat him as what he is, he will remain what he is."

That's as good a guidance as any on how to develop players, or anyone else, to their full potential. Pascal Siakam is probably the most notable example of our player development efforts, though he is just one of many. Fred VanVleet is another.

I had been working closely with both of them since they came to the Raptors in 2016, when I was still an assistant coach. In each of their cases, when they entered the league, there was a lot written and said about their (supposed) limits—and less about their potential.

Pascal got a late start playing basketball for a couple of reasons. He thought for a time he might become a Catholic priest in his native Cameroon. And when he did play sports, his preferred game was soccer.

But he was tall—he's six foot nine now—and he finally began playing basketball in his mid-teens. At fifteen, he was discovered at a camp near his home that was being run by Luc Mbah a Moute, another Cameroonian, who was then just starting out on what would become a twelve-year NBA career. The next year, Masai Ujiri took notice of Pascal at a Basketball Without Borders camp in Africa.

At sixteen, Pascal moved to Texas for prep school and then

went on to play for New Mexico State. He did well, averaging twenty points and almost twelve rebounds in his final season. It's fair to say that scouts were impressed by him but not exactly blown away.

There were some concerns that Pascal's college team rarely played against strong competition, which put his statistics into doubt. The bloggers who write about the NBA draft chimed in with other critiques, one of them being his "advanced" age compared to other prospective picks.

He "turned 22 in January so there is some question about his upside," is how one put it. He was referred to as an "energy guy"—which is usually a shorthand way of describing an athletic player without great skills who can chip in ten or twelve minutes off the bench while a starter is resting.

You can't take these things too seriously, of course. Another of the draft sites, when listing Pascal's "comps"—former or present NBA players whose skills he mirrored—named Luc Mbah a Moute as his closest match. Why? No idea, but maybe because they are both from Cameroon?

The pre-draft commentary, though, did more or less predict Pascal's fate on draft night. We were able to select him with the twenty-seventh pick—meaning after almost the whole league had passed on him.

When *Sports Illustrated* issued its "grades" for each team, they didn't think our pick of him scored out particularly well. We only got a C-plus, and *SI* repeated some of the concerns about Pascal—too old, not a great shooter, nothing more than an energy guy.

Pascal was someone who, right from the start, we saw as having a lot of room for growth. There's a real grace to him as an athlete. He covers vast amounts of territory without seeming to exert himself, but then you look up and see that he's beaten everyone else down the floor and is catching a pass for an easy basket.

A player can stay in the league a long time and make a lot of money just competing with that kind of energy, but we knew there was more to Pascal. In college, he played almost exclusively close to the hoop, and he was good at it, which is why if you watch him now, he's got great moves in the post. He's basically unguardable down low if teams put a smaller player on him.

But his evolution into an even bigger offensive threat had to come from taking his game out away from the basket, so that if teams defended him with a bigger player, he could take advantage of his quickness. But he also had to learn to shoot the ball from out there.

The first season we got swept by the Cavaliers, 2016–17, was Pascal's rookie season. He averaged four points a game, and then when the playoffs came around, he barely played. He got into just two games for a total of ten minutes and didn't score a single point.

It was after that series that I feared we were all going to get fired—when management called us all in and said no one was going anywhere for a while. It was a panicked deal. They said we had to get better as a team. We had to coach better. Make the guys we already have better. Make them into championship players. They said we needed to get together with them before they got out of town and make clear what they had to do to improve.

Pascal's shot needed to be totally rebuilt. He was starting it by winding it around from his left side, and that's probably what he had been doing since he first picked up a ball in Cameroon.

A lot of players develop habits when they are not strong enough to get the ball up to the hoop, and those idiosyncrasies follow them right into professional basketball. They have a comfort with their style—an attitude that it's just the way they shoot—and when they've got enough other skills to dominate at lower levels, nobody tries to change them.

And many times, they are resistant to change. Pascal did not have that issue. He came into the gym the day that season ended, and I remember him saying to me, "I need to learn how to shoot."

I went over to a basket with him and gave him a marked-up ball. I had put a stripe on it so he could square himself up correctly. It was like I was running shooting camps again, and we were working with the Nurse's Pill, or a version of it. I said, "Here's your workout: Take 150 of these shots from three feet, with this new way I'm showing you. Take a hundred free throws, a hundred corner three-pointers, and a hundred three-pointers from the top of the arc."

Most of it is just mechanics. Most important, the ball has to come off your hand consistently, the same every time. It can't go right and it can't go left. It can be long or short, but if it's wide, you're doing something wrong.

You have to groove the proper form and then be able to repeat it every time, like a golf swing—except in golf, there's not a six-foot-eight guy flying at you just as you're about to complete the process.

A couple of days later, Pascal left Toronto and went to Orlando, where he was living in the off-season, and he was doing this twice a day. He came back the next season and we just kept encouraging, pushing him to do more.

In the following season, Pascal's second in the league—and my last as an assistant, before stepping into the head coaching role—

we were looking at film one day. It was just a regular postgame edit, but I added a little something extra.

I said to the team, "I've got one little addition here I want to show." And I put up six clips of Pascal doing things from the night before—grabbing a rebound and going coast-to-coast, pulling up and nailing a three-pointer. And I said, "We're going to encourage him to play like this, just so everybody knows, right, what he's capable of?" And everybody loved it.

What he did not improve, right away, was his shooting. He took a bunch of three-pointers and he hardly made any. He was like two for thirty at one point, something really awful. All we said was, "Keep shooting them."

∧

The championship year was Pascal's third season in the NBA, and a breakout one for him. He became what we had hoped for and what he had been working toward: a multidimensional threat.

He connected on 37 percent of his three-point shots, which opened up the whole rest of the floor for him. He was no longer just an "energy guy." He was a highly skilled basketball player who also happened to be a superior athlete.

There was another part of his development still to tend to: Could we make him into a player who had the ball in his hands when we needed a basket in late-game situations? And would he embrace that responsibility? What we were asking had as much to do with grit, his mental toughness, as it did with physical ability.

Pascal actually had gotten off to a slow start. In six of the first ten games, he scored ten points or fewer. In two of them, he scored four points. Kawhi was, in some ways, a similar player—

they occupied some of the same parts of the court—and Pascal may have been deferring a bit.

But he picked up his scoring as the season progressed, and interestingly, a lot of his bigger games did not come when Kawhi was resting. The two were complementing each other and they became dual threats.

It had been in the back of my mind to spread the end-of-game scenarios around a little bit, and there were some opportunities, but in the heat of the moment, I went in a different direction. After each one, I thought: maybe next time.

In mid-January, the Phoenix Suns came into Toronto. They would end up with the worst record in the Western Conference, and we played, frankly, a crappy game—one of those dead-of-winter affairs when the season feels a little long, the playoffs are still a ways off, and you play down to your competition. We blew a couple of big leads, trailed briefly near the end of the fourth quarter, and with thirteen seconds left on the clock, were in a 109–109 tie and inbounding the ball at half-court.

Pascal had not played particularly well up to that point. He had eight points on just seven shot attempts. Kyle was really cold—four for fifteen from the floor and he had even missed three foul shots. He did get his five-thousandth career assist that night, which was a cool moment. (It put him fifty-seventh on the all-time NBA list, but if he stays healthy, he should easily climb into the top twenty before he's done, or even the top ten.)

I think I said something quickly to Kyle about giving the last shot to Pascal, and he was good, so we rolled with it. In the huddle, I said to get Pascal the ball in the middle of the floor and just basically get the hell out of the way. We might have set some kind of quick screen just to make it look like we were running something, but we weren't. I wanted him to dribble the clock down and take a shot with the buzzer going off.

We got him the ball right where we intended. He was guarded by Mikal Bridges, a six-foot-seven rookie the Suns selected in the first round because he is a rangy, tough defender. As the clock wound down, Pascal beat him off the dribble and drove to the hoop. The Suns' center, six-foot-eleven Deandre Ayton, jumped to try to block the shot (and also gave Pascal a forceful shove in the midsection with his forearm), but Pascal got it off over him, with his left hand. The ball banked off the backboard and fell through the hoop just as the clock hit zero.

One reason you want multiple options late in the game is it makes your team less predictable. The opposing team comes out of the huddle assuming a certain player will take the shot and you can cross them up. After Pascal's shot, the Suns coach at the time, Igor Kokoškov, said, "We were surprised...I was thinking Lowry was going to take the last shot."

Those opportunities do not come up that much, and even the great players miss the shot as often as they make it. The thing they all have to get over is the fear of failure—of being the guy walking off the court with the cameras on him as teammates give him those little consoling pats on the back. It's not a good feeling, but to take the big shot, you have to be willing to endure it.

The media in Toronto made a big deal of Pascal's last-second shot and there was lots of talk about him taking a big step forward in his development, finally growing up as a player, and all that kind of stuff. I still get asked about it.

It was a big moment for our team, because in addition to Kawhi and Kyle, the obvious late-game threats, we had added a third player to the mix. Pascal was the least excited of anyone. As

I recall, he said something along the lines of, "What's everybody tripping about?"

We had fixed his shooting form, but the courage to take a big shot was already in him when he got to us.

^

Fred VanVleet was in the same draft class as Pascal—except that he was not drafted at all. Sixty players were deemed more worthy.

(The NBA draft is two rounds, with thirty players picked in each. Because of trades, we had two first-round picks in 2016—before we picked Pascal, we selected Jakob Poeltl, with the seventh overall pick, who after two seasons with the Raptors was dealt to San Antonio in the trade that brought us Kawhi Leonard.)

In terms of his attractiveness to the league's talent scouts, Fred had one of the same issues as Pascal: he was old. And by that, I mean he had just turned twenty-two.

He played four years at Wichita State in an era when all the top prospects—the players whom NBA scouts value highest—leave college after just one year, or two at the most. To stay for all four years generally means that in the NBA's collective opinion, you are a non-prospect.

Fred's other challenge was that he did not look the part, and to be honest, he still doesn't. He is listed at an even six feet tall and is kind of rounded in his build. If you passed him on the street, he's not someone you would notice and think, *Oh, wow, that guy is probably a pro athlete.* Maybe you would clock him as an accountant—or the guy who fits you for sneakers at Foot Locker.

The reviews Fred got from the draft "experts" were mostly negative, bordering on withering. "Below average size and length," one wrote, adding, "below average tools." "Struggles to get his shot off at the rim." He also got some pats on the back from the experts. "Peppery" point guard was one of them, along with the old "coach on the floor" compliment.

But Dan Tolzman, our assistant general manager, had seen Fred play numerous times at Wichita State and he loved him. He brought him to Toronto before the draft for a private work-out, and when he did not get selected, we signed him as a free agent.

As the head coach, I have, at most, a small voice in whom we draft—or in Fred's case, whom we decide to sign as an undrafted free agent. I'll jump in and have an opinion, but there are other guys who have been out there scouting and evaluating all year long and they've got a lot more basis for their judgments. As an assistant coach, which is what I was the year Fred came out of college, I had no voice.

But just generally, I do have a high regard for guys who played on winning teams, who started a lot of games, and who won championships. When he first came to us, the one thing we knew for sure about Fred was that he's a winner. In his sophomore season at Wichita State, he was the point guard and leader on a squad that went 35-0 during the regular season. His teams over his four seasons were a combined 121-24. We tend to get really caught up in a guy's measurements—height and wing-span, or his vertical leap—but all that winning should count for something.

Sometimes you have to wait for players. As a rookie, Fred did not get into his first game until we were a couple of weeks into the season. He played twenty-six seconds. He didn't score a point until December. He spent a lot of that season bouncing back and forth between the Raptors and our D-League team.

But the more he played for us, the more people saw this incredible knack he has for driving against bigger people and getting a shot up under them, around them, over them—from all kinds of odd angles—and still getting it in the basket. He throws his torso into people and makes more layups than any player his size I've seen. I feel like I can explain just about any damn thing about basketball, but I'm not sure I can really say how Fred scores so many close-in baskets. (Interestingly, Kyle, basically the same size as Fred, has the same knack. I'm sure it drives other teams crazy to see both of our little guys shoot all those layups.)

Fred's outside shot was good when he came to us and continues to improve. On defense, he is tireless—and extremely smart.

The concept of "athleticism" in basketball—what Fred supposedly lacked—is open to question, or at least to some deeper thought. People generally just mean size or speed or jumping ability and they discount the finer skills of shot-making—and the ability to anticipate the action and make a play on offense or defense.

Fred has joked about his lack of athletic ability. After a game in which he scored twenty-one points and dished out eleven assists, he told reporters, "The only thing I haven't done yet is dunk...I dunk in the summer every once in a while. It's gotta be like a certain amount of right degrees outside and the gym's gotta have the right humidity...I don't know if you'll see it from me this year. Don't hold your breath."

We are far from the only team around the league to successfully develop players. Draymond Green of the Golden State Warriors was a second-round draft pick. So were a couple of rising stars, Malcolm Brogdon of the Indiana Pacers and Nikola Jokić of the Denver Nuggets. There are many other examples of players picked near the end of the draft, or not drafted at all, who have made a big impact.

In the case of Pascal and Fred (and more recently, another undrafted prospect who landed with us, Terrence Davis), credit goes first to the players. Yes, we saw something in them, but it was what they already knew. They had that conviction, deep down, that they could make it in the NBA. They're the ones who put in the work, the long hours in the gym.

But we were not deterred by their body types or any other perceived negative metrics. We saw something we liked, gave them an opportunity, and provided a framework they could fit into and succeed in.

One other player on our championship roster could be described as a triumph of player development—or maybe more accurately, player *redevelopment*. We didn't build Kawhi Leonard. He did that himself, as all players ultimately do—with help from his youth coaches, his coaches at San Diego State, and head coach Gregg Popovich and his staff with the San Antonio Spurs.

But we definitely did help rebuild him.

Kawhi's first six NBA seasons were mostly, but not entirely, healthy ones. He averaged sixty-six games a year, so he always missed some due to various injuries. It was definitely not for lack of conditioning on his part. He works out the same way he plays—like a machine. He's totally dedicated and focused on working on his body, but he came to us after that knee injury had robbed him of almost the entire previous season. He missed seventy-three games and all five of the Spurs' playoff games. His season ended on January 13.

Over the years, many other NBA players, especially veteran stars, have been given games off to rest, especially late in seasons with the playoffs looming. Sometimes minor injuries were cited.

What was different in Kawhi's case is that we defined a program at the beginning of the season. He was not going to play both games when we were scheduled on back-to-back nights. All through the season, we were going to closely monitor his minutes.

Our goal was to keep him healthy during the regular season and have him available and at full strength for the playoffs. Alex McKechnie put a name on our approach, which is now being used by other teams: load management.

The practice is controversial, and I understand why. NBA fans pay a lot of money for tickets and they're disappointed if they show up and one of the marquee players is resting. The league has since adopted some guidelines that prohibit teams from sitting healthy players in certain "high-profile" nationally televised games. It requires that they be rested only at home, except under "unusual circumstances," since fans in other cities may have only one or two opportunities to see certain players.

When we first started out, we said Kawhi wouldn't play back-to-backs. There were benchmarks on how many total minutes he would play. We were going to reassess in December and maybe loosen up some of the restrictions. But they were working, and we figured, let's just keep it rolling. We're playing well and he's in good shape. After one really busy stretch in mid-January, we decided to just let him rest and he missed four games.

What we did was best for our team, for Kawhi, and, I think, ultimately for the league and its fans. It allowed one of the NBA's best players to stay healthy during the season and then right through the final game of the playoffs.

The way we used him was based on a lot of communication, first to set the plan and make sure it felt right to him. It continued through the season and even in the midst of games. We were always mindful of the goal not to play him more than ten minutes at a stretch.

At times, there might be 9:30 left in the fourth quarter and I'd turn to him, and he'd say, "I need another minute and a half." And that would be fine, because even if we were down six points, I knew when he came back, he would be fully ready. He knew how to really gear up for the last five or six minutes of a game.

Other times, it was a bit of a negotiation. I'd say, "We really need to change what's going on here. We can't wait." And I'd tell him that if we could get him back in the game immediately, I'd get him another break around the two-minute mark. He would take that short breather and then jump back in.

Kawhi was in as good—or better—condition than anyone out there. But we were focused on him not breaking down.

It might surprise some people to hear this, but he ended up averaging thirty-four minutes per game during the regular season—a career high. (He played sixty out of the eighty-two games.) He either set new career highs or was right on his peak performances in just about everything else down the stat line—points, rebounds, field goal and foul shot attempts. When he was on the court, he was more dynamic and efficient than he had ever been.

His playing time was a collaboration between the two of us, in close consultation with the front office and medical staff. The relationship was comfortable, and I felt like we were using him just right—physically, mentally, and situationally. It was another thing that we were able to try out during the season and practice and refine it for when we would need to do it perfectly.

⌃

One of the biggest challenges of coaching in the NBA is finding moments during the season to actually coach. You often have to do so without having much of an opportunity for running what might seem like a normal practice.

After we play, we usually fly on to the next city that same night—either back to Toronto or to a stop on the road. It's common to arrive in the middle of the night, like three-thirty A.M. And then we normally play again within thirty-six hours. On average, NBA teams play every 2.07 days. Thirteen times a year, we play on back-to-back nights.

A story on the ESPN website last fall explored the phenomenon of sleep deprivation as a league-wide problem and described players' elaborate efforts to get in enough hours. (LeBron James was said to set his phone so it "serenades him with the soothing sound of rain falling on leaves.")

I usually can get very little out of the players on the day after a game. If we have practice, it's hit or miss if it's going to be worth it. They are ready to give you something on the day of the game, which is when we have what the NBA has long called "shootarounds." They were designed, I believe, to get players out of bed, out of the hotel, and moving around on game days, but now they serve as an important time to do some game prep.

Even so, we keep them to under an hour. And not to get too deep in the weeds here, but there are also challenges with traffic to and from practice sites in a lot of cities—you can end up on a bus for ninety minutes round-trip for a forty-five-minute shootaround. The players come back to the hotel and a few hours later, they're back on the bus to go to the game.

In New York, sometimes we do a shootaround in a gym at the Manhattan headquarters of the NBA Players Association. It's undersized, but convenient.

We'll usually do a film session at the hotel on the morning of an away game, twenty minutes or so. At the arena, exactly thirty-two minutes before a game, we look at a little more film of our opponent. Their offensive sets, out-of-bounds plays, maybe one other thing we want to highlight.

And that's it. Some shootarounds and the film sessions can be the bulk of our coaching over the course of a week or two—maybe with one or two real practices slipped in.

A season kind of exists on two levels. At times, it feels like a slog with all the travel and games on top of each other. But the overall feeling is that it sort of whizzes by.

Our championship season felt like it started in turmoil, with like seven fires going at once. I was new and trying to mesh my style with those of several new assistant coaches. We were working to integrate Kawhi, with all that entailed—and also waiting out whatever ruffled feelings remained over the trade of DeMar DeRozan to pass.

It was probably a good lesson going forward—to not worry too much about change and what sometimes feels like friction. You ride it out. You grow from it.

It all came together as the regular season moved forward. We had that three-game losing streak in November (the one where Kawhi spoke up against the idea of just passing the ball around for the hell of it) but would never lose that many in a row again the rest of the season.

Our big in-season move was the trade for Marc Gasol. We gave up our starting center, Jonas Valančiūnas, who was in his eighth year with the Raptors—along with CJ Miles and point guard Delon Wright, both of whom were getting playing time off the bench.

It was a pretty big shake-up and not universally applauded as a move that was going to propel us forward. A story in *Sports Illustrated* offered the following opinion: "Marc Gasol helps, but he's lost a step defensively, and it's not even clear he'd be part of the best Toronto lineup in the playoffs. Meanwhile, in the past three months, the Raptors have gone from the clear favorites in the East to arguably the least imposing playoff team of the big four (Boston, Philly, Milwaukee, Toronto)."

The truth was that Marc, at thirty-four years old, was still an elite defensive player. In addition, there might be no player in the league who would be an easier fit, midseason, on a new team. At seven feet tall, he is a skilled passer as well as a "pass-first" player—someone who looks to set up his teammates to score before looking for his own shots. (Sometimes you need to beg him to shoot.)

I coached against him years ago in Europe and was a big fan. He's the kind of player teammates love playing with, and he completed our group. We were a good passing team that became a great passing team.

Over the course of the regular season, we put together a series of winning streaks, and as soon as one would end, we'd start on another. We had two winning streaks of five games, two six-game streaks, and a seven- and an eight-game streak. We finished the regular season 58-24—one win less than the previous season.

Only one team in the league had more wins—the Milwaukee Bucks, with sixty.

But even so, we did not enter the postseason as one of the favorites to win the title. I feel like we were regarded in about the same way as we were at the start of the year. *Pretty nice team. Maybe they'll go a couple of rounds in the playoffs before the big boys take the stage.*

⌃

12

ORLANDO AND ONWARD

THE PLAYOFFS ARRIVE

Arguing a foul call with Fred VanVleet. *(Harry How / Getty Images)*

If I look at it honestly, I was probably one of the biggest question marks. First-year NBA coach. Had only been an assistant in the league five years, all with the same team. Thrown into the cauldron of the NBA playoffs with a roster that did not look all that much different than the one that had underachieved in past postseasons.

I made it clear right at the start by handing out those AMJ bracelets: We would measure ourselves by how we did in the postseason. A maximum of four series and twenty-eight games (about 34 percent as long as the NBA's regular season schedule) stretching from April all the way into mid-June.

We began on April 13 against the Orlando Magic at Scotiabank Arena in Toronto. As usual, it was filled to its nearly twenty-thousand-seat capacity. You could feel that different kind of playoff atmosphere in the building. It's hard to put into words but it's a higher level of excitement, for sure, with a layer of nervousness running through it—maybe especially in Toronto because of our history.

As a franchise, we had a bad habit of losing the first game of a playoff series—and often at home, thereby squandering the home court advantage we had worked all year to earn. Overall, the Raptors had been in fifteen previous playoff series and lost the first game thirteen times.

Well, guess what? We came out in Game 1 against Orlando like we were half-asleep.

We played with a modest lead through most of the first quarter and then started gifting the Magic with open shots all over the floor. We have certain ways we want to defend, depending on who the opponent is and what we talk about before a game. We looked like we had forgotten it all from the moment we walked out of the locker room.

On offense, I barely recognized whatever we were trying to do. A play near the end of the first half typified our performance. As he was trying to back a defender down on the right side of the lane, Kawhi picked up his dribble—he wasn't even double-teamed—and just floated a pass back out to the perimeter. I think it was intended for Kyle. The Magic easily intercepted it and ended up with a dunk at the other end, pushing their lead to sixteen points, 57–41.

We clawed back in the second half and the game went back and forth, but we never did look particularly good. In the fourth quarter, with the score tied at 101 and four seconds left on the clock, their point guard, DJ Augustin, had the ball near the top of the three-point arc. He got a screen—Kawhi and Marc Gasol got their wires crossed on the coverage we were in—and left Augustin unguarded.

Augustin calmly raised up for a wide-open shot and nailed it. It would have been surprising if he missed. He was so wide open he could have been in the gym by himself.

Kawhi got a shot opportunity at the other end to tie it. It wasn't a bad look, but it did not even hit the rim. The ball just bounced out of bounds—a fitting end for our performance that evening.

⌃

I wrote about my vow that I would fire only six "bullets" over the course of the season—six times I'd really let loose on the team. I had not used them all, not even close. It rarely felt necessary. But this was definitely a moment.

That first game against Orlando was on a Saturday night and the next one was not until Tuesday, which, considering what had happened, felt like an eternity. I figured I'd just let it sink in for twenty-four hours so they could think about it. The next day at practice, I didn't have that much to say. I just sat there calmly, listening to everybody. The general consensus, it seemed to me, was that everything was going to be okay.

Players like to muddy the waters. When things go wrong, they'll find excuses—blame the refs, try to lay some mix-up or another on a teammate—and I heard a little of that.

The Toronto media killed us, and I didn't blame them. TORONTO RAPTORS' GAME 1 LOSS TO ORLANDO MAGIC SETS A TERRIBLE FIRST IMPRESSION—ONE THAT WILL LAST read a headline in the *Globe and Mail.* Another story said that despite the moves we had made—the coaching change, the trade for Kawhi, and the midseason deal for Gasol—it still looked like we might not be able to "prevent being the laughingstock of the Eastern Conference elites in the playoffs yet again."

Kyle Lowry came in for some really tough criticism. We had successfully decreased his minutes the last couple of years, and I thought he entered the postseason fresh and ready to go, but he was somehow held scoreless. That *Globe and Mail* article said that he "played 34 minutes and did not score a single point. That is so unusual in basketball, it's almost an achievement." His counterpart, DJ Augustin, scored twenty-five.

We had a film session on that Monday where I planned to show selected clips from the previous game—the lowlights of all the dumb stuff we did. I took Kyle into my office beforehand and said, "We're going to work our way out of this."

I wanted to acknowledge to him that I was in it with him. I was getting a lot of shit, too, for getting outcoached. That was the word—that I had proven I wasn't ready for prime time.

I said to Kyle, "This is why we get paid a lot of money, because sometimes we just have to take it."

"I got you," Kyle said, meaning we would pick each other up.

"Okay, then, get ready in the film room today, because I'm fucking pissed," I said. "You know what I mean?"

"And you should be," Kyle said as he got up and walked out.

⌃

After lying back all season, I was running the film sessions. That was my plan all along, but I didn't anticipate I'd have to really lay into them the moment we began the playoffs.

I showed sixteen clips that day. I remember that I started hitting the screen with my finger sort of lightly. By the end, I was pounding on it.

I was really giving it to Kawhi, Kyle, Marc, and Danny Green. Four veterans. I didn't have that much to say to Pascal, who had asserted himself and scored twenty-four points. And besides, he was a young guy and not the one I was counting on to lead us and get everyone over whatever anxiety they were feeling.

I remember showing Augustin running all over us and saying, "This guy...*this guy*...*this* is the guy that we let beat us." I didn't mean any disrespect at all to DJ, a really solid and smart player who was in his eleventh NBA season (including ten games with the Raptors in 2013), but he had never averaged more than fifteen points a game, and that was back in 2011. In his previous playoff appearances, he scored at a six-point-a-game clip.

We made him look unguardable, like he was Allen Iverson and

we couldn't keep up with him. My point was that if our goal was to advance deep into the playoffs—where we would likely face players like Joel Embiid and Giannis Antetokounmpo, and if we got to the Finals, probably Steph Curry, Kevin Durant, and Klay Thompson—we were never going to make it if we couldn't guard DJ Augustin.

We watch film in a nice amphitheater—stadium seating, plenty of room for everyone's long legs—but it was uncomfortable in there. I told them something to the effect of, "Everybody is telling us it's going to be okay and it's only going to be okay if we fucking make it okay, you know what I mean?"

It was high volume, high intensity. A lot of f-bombs. We had not played hard enough. Half-assed. Disjointed.

I honestly didn't know what happened, but I needed to change it, and quickly. I had not been nervous all season, but I was really anxious going into the next game, probably because the way we played was such a mystery to me. I didn't see it coming.

But you can't really know the true nature of your team until the playoffs. Everything gets ratcheted up. Some guys rise to a new level and others don't. Did I have enough players who were going to step up, or was this going to be another Raptors nosedive?

I hadn't coached Kawhi in the postseason before. I knew he had another gear from his playoff performances in San Antonio, but was that still physically in him? And was he going to give it to us or just move on to the next team?

I was fairly certain I knew the answer. He had been competitive as hell for us. He had not seemed to hold anything back. But I wasn't going to feel better until I saw it, because we were not getting far without him.

Thirteen seconds into Game 2, Kawhi dribbled to his left, stopped at the foul line, and swished a jump shot. A couple of minutes later, he hit another from a little closer in. A moment after that, he stole a pass, dribbled full court, and with two defenders trying to stop him, dribbled behind his back, stopped on a dime, and nailed another jump shot.

He scored ten of our first eighteen points and would finish the game with thirty-seven, in just thirty-three minutes on the court. Several of his buckets were midrange jumpers, the kind that our shot spectrum discourages, but Kawhi is an exception to that rule. He easily rises up over defenders, gets those shots off, and hits a high percentage of them.

He connected on four three-pointers that night. His stroke was pure and effortless and few of his shots hit anything but net. Kyle righted himself and scored twenty-two points.

On defense, we gave them nothing. We closely guarded the ball and had our long arms in the passing lanes all night. We had ten steals and a ton of deflections. (All NBA teams now count deflections, which often are as good as steals because they disrupt an offense and take time off the twenty-four-second clock.)

And we solved our DJ Augustin problem. He managed just one bucket on six shot attempts.

We scored the game's first eleven points, never once trailed, and won, 111–82. We totally dominated them all over the floor, especially defensively. I saw enough that game to know how good we could be in playoff mode. Going forward, we would hit some bumps—and have our backs against the wall a couple of times— but I never had that uneasy feeling again entering a game.

They showed me that night what was possible. I told them in the locker room afterward, "If you can play like that, you can go anywhere you want to go."

We took care of the Magic with three consecutive wins to finish off the series, mainly because our defense stayed extremely strong: the Magic averaged just ninety-one points the rest of the series.

In the next round, the semifinals of the Eastern Conference, we were matched up against the Philadelphia 76ers. We finished the regular season with seven more wins than they did, so we began in Toronto, and would play four of the games at home if the series went the distance.

The big news was that we did *not* lose the first game. Kawhi, who was absolutely dominant—forty-five points on sixteen-of-twenty-three shooting—made sure of that. But we did lose the next two, so once again we were playing from behind and in a pretty desperate spot.

I am going to focus for a moment on the third game—which was the first in Philly after we split in Toronto. I refer to it as the "airplane game" because their star, center Joel Embiid, kept running around with his arms angled up, like a jetliner, after every great play he made.

And he made a lot of great plays. He scored thirty-three points, grabbed ten rebounds, and blocked five of our shots. As their home crowd got into his airplane routine, he would turn his palms upward, signaling that they needed to increase the volume.

Embiid is a monumentally gifted player—massive, at seven feet tall and 280 pounds, with great strength and quickness, unusually nimble footwork for a man that big, and a nice shooting touch. But he also plays off emotion, and that was what I addressed after our loss. (If you watch the television replay of the airplane game, you hear a commentator say, "Boy, he's enjoying it tonight!")

We went to the arena in Philly to practice. I did not say to the team that we were in a must-win situation because that's how TV commentators and fans talk. I also did not say it because it was obvious. It's possible to come back from a 3–1 hole but it only happens about once every ten years in the NBA.

After the players warmed up, I called everybody off the floor and into the locker room. I didn't rip into them. In my opinion, what we needed was a plan.

I had a dry-erase board and I drew a line down the middle—defense on one side, offense on the other. I said, "Okay, we're going to talk about the problems we've got."

And then I drew a line underneath, a separate category, and I said, "This is the other thing we're going to address. Joel Embiid."

Every NBA team has a substitution pattern. A coach may change it up later in games, as the situation dictates, but early on, it stays consistent. The Sixers' routine was that Embiid came out for a rest five minutes into the first quarter.

I wanted him to go to the bench that first time with nothing to feel good about. I said to our team, "Listen, Embiid's a different player if he doesn't get off to a good start. He rides the crowd. Here's what we're going to do. For that first five minutes, until they sub him out, every time he catches it in the post, we're sending everybody. We're not letting him get a shot off, okay?"

The Sixers' other big threat, Jimmy Butler, had been hurting us at the end of games, when he became their primary ball handler. Embiid set screens for him, and Butler had a way of slithering into the lane for short jump shots—or getting all the way to the hoop for layups and dunks.

I told them, "On screen-and-rolls, we're not helping—we're not coming off Embiid to stop Butler. I understand what this means. Butler may get some open shots. But listen, for this part of the game, we live with it. Embiid wants to roll and create havoc and we're not going to let him. I'm going to get to how we want to defend Butler in a minute. But in this first stretch of the game, I don't care what he does. I don't care what the rest of their guys do. I just want us to keep Embiid quiet."

The following night, five minutes and four seconds into the game, we committed a foul and there was a stoppage of play. Like clockwork, the Sixers coach, Brett Brown, subbed for Embiid. Our strategy held him just as quiet as I hoped. He had one rebound and one assist. He attempted one shot, which he missed.

That put us on the course I wanted, though the game—and, in fact, the rest of the series—was hardly a cakewalk. In this must-win Game 4, we were up three points at the end of the first quarter, up two at the half, and tied, 77–77, going into the fourth quarter.

We scratched out a very hard-fought 101–96 victory to tie the series. Kawhi had seven points in the last four minutes and finished the game with thirty-nine.

Embiid never got going. He finished with only eleven points, on two-of-seven shooting. The rest of his points were from the foul line.

If you want to be known as a brilliant coach, my number one recommendation would be to surround yourself with really smart players. You can dream stuff up with your assistants all you want—schemes to stop the other team's top scorers or get your own squad great shots—but it will make no difference if your players don't have the aptitude to execute the plan.

The team we had in 2018–19 was incredibly smart, from Kawhi to Marc to Kyle to Serge. Pascal and Freddy were younger and less experienced, but you would have never known it.

Embiid is a handful and you just can't keep defending him the same way every time. Ben Simmons presents unique challenges as an extremely oversized (six-foot-ten) point guard. Jimmy Butler is a late-game assassin. You can do everything right and he might still beat you.

We double-teamed Embiid from three different spots on the floor and kept changing it up. Depending on where we sent the second player from, our rotations (how the other players compensate for the double team) kept changing. We did it on the fly and kept altering it.

We'd talk about it in the huddle during a time-out. I'd have a thought—a lot of times, the players would have a different thought, then we would come together with a plan. It was a total collaboration. As a coach, it was deeply satisfying, because the players were thinking right along with me.

The other Sixers player we had to worry about was JJ Redick, one of the most prolific three-point shooters in NBA history. Normally, you would set up your rotations to give special attention to him and make sure he doesn't get shots. But we said, no, we're going to play him honest and just work our asses off to get back and fly at him when he has a shot.

Redick has a unique style—he can zoom around at like a hundred miles an hour, point himself toward the right corner, catch the ball on the run, and bang shots. Unlike most shooters, he does not need his feet set under him. He hits shots as he's flying out of bounds.

Redick had a special connection with Embiid, who got him the ball in those situations, often with what we call dribble handoffs. One thing we tried was to just not let Embiid turn in a direction where he could put the ball in Redick's hands.

Some of what we did worked. When it didn't, we would quickly come out of it and try something different. Like all great NBA playoff series, our competition against the 76ers was in part a chess match. Move. Countermove.

In the fifth game back in Toronto, we took a lead late in the first quarter and just pulled away from there for a 125–89 victory. We stopped Embiid again in his first stretch of play—no baskets, one made free throw—and he finished the game with just thirteen points.

It wasn't just team defense or a clever strategy that stopped Embiid. It all started with Marc Gasol. He was physical with Embiid. He didn't get pushed around, and he used his leverage to prevent Embiid from setting up in his favorite spots.

From the airplane game forward, Embiid would make only eighteen of his forty-nine shot attempts—which is 37 percent, or twelve percentage points worse than during the regular season. He averaged sixteen points a game in the series against us, twelve off his average during the year.

Our decision to swarm him early in games was more successful than I could have hoped. Over the course of the final four games—in twenty-one combined minutes before he was subbed out—Embiid scored a total of three points on one-of-nine shooting.

The series, however, reverted to one in which the home team held serve, as it's sometimes said. After we coasted in Toronto in Game 5, the Sixers evened the series up two days later with a 112–101 victory in Philly. We had a horrible shooting night—nine for thirty-six (25 percent) on our three-point attempts—

and the final score made the game seem a little closer than it really was.

That set up a decisive Game 7—a game that will forever be known in Toronto for the Shot.

⌃

It was a typical seventh game. Everything was contested. Players with the ball barely had room to breathe—and neither team shot it well because good shots were hard to come by.

Some shots that did go in you would categorize as having a high degree of difficulty—made possible only by the skill of NBA players. Kawhi connected on a reverse, spinning, double-pump, left-handed layup in the first half that was just ridiculous. Kyle got himself room on one drive into the lane by hurling his body into a Sixers defender, and he ended up with the hoop and a foul shot. Those were the kind of efforts it took to score.

The game was close from start to finish, but about halfway through the third quarter, we almost lost a little contact with them. Redick hit a three-pointer and Jimmy Butler followed with two free throws to give them a seven-point lead—which on that night felt like a lot.

But we quickly caught up, though we never built a comfortable lead. For the whole last sixteen minutes of the game, the score was within five points.

You don't hold anything back in a game like that. Marc Gasol played forty-five of the forty-eight minutes. Kawhi played forty-three, and Lowry and Siakam also played heavy minutes. I played only two guys off the bench—Serge Ibaka and Fred VanVleet. The Sixers used three subs, but one played less than three minutes.

The atmosphere was crazy, like nothing I had ever been a part of. A lot of our fans were out of their seats and cheering or chanting the entire last quarter. They never sat down.

On the court, it seemed that on every possession, at least one player ended up sprawled on the floor. Sometimes it was two or three. Guys at that point had thrown so much of themselves into the effort that they could not fathom losing. It's what I meant when I said that younger players cannot understand how hard they have to play until they've been through it.

We were totally locked in and determined on defense. We pressured the ball. We corralled the right guys with two defenders and then quickly scrambled back to the player we had just left open.

Kyle, particularly, was all over the place—every time he saw them with an opening, he came off his man and took it away. In one three-and-a-half-minute span right at the end, we held them without a basket, although Butler and Embiid combined to make four foul shots.

With twelve seconds left in the game, we had a 89–88 lead when Redick fouled Kawhi and sent him to the line for two shots. If Kawhi hit them both, it would be a three-point lead and the Sixers would need either a three-pointer—or a quick two-pointer and some mistakes by us—to tie it. It was possible, but if he sank both foul shots, we would make it really hard on them.

Kawhi, an excellent foul shooter, made the first but came up short on the second. Marc Gasol got his left hand on the rebound as the ball came off the front of the rim and batted it out toward the foul line. The Sixers' Tobias Harris came up with it and quickly passed it to their most decisive player, Jimmy Butler.

Butler was still short of half-court, but he never looked at anyone else. He drove the ball down the right side, split two defenders, and laid the ball in high off the backboard and over Serge's outstretched right hand. That tied it at 90.

Pascal might have been able to step in and help, but he was drifting toward the right corner, where Redick was in position to shoot a three. It was the right decision because you would rather be tied at that point than down one.

We had 4.4 seconds left to score or the game would go to overtime. I knew that Kawhi was pissed that he missed the foul shot. Up until that point, he had attempted an extraordinary number of shots from the field—thirty-eight—almost half the number we had taken as a team and three times as many as his closest teammate.

If you just looked at the box score, you might think he had taken too many shots, but with the suffocating defense being played, Kawhi was the one guy we had who was physically able to get himself a decent shot when all else broke down.

We were going to inbound the ball from half-court, on the left sideline. I did not consult with any of my assistants before setting up a play; I knew what I wanted to call. We had given a couple of different guys end-of-game shots during the season—I wrote earlier about Pascal succeeding in that role—but it had to be Kawhi at this point with the ball in his hands.

It's what everyone in the arena expected, but it was one of those moments when the obvious move is the right move. I was not looking to surprise anyone. (Fred said later that he was thinking, "Kawhi's gonna get the ball? I mean, that's what he's here for, right?")

I grabbed the board and drew up what we call our "4" sideline out-of-bounds play. I got it from a Hubie Brown DVD back in 2007 and have been running it forever, since my Iowa Energy days. We did not have our starters out there—Serge was in for

Danny—so I had to quickly make sure everyone knew where they should line up. (And say it really loud over the noise in the arena.)

I drew it up so that Marc Gasol, a cool head and reliable passer, would throw the inbounds pass. At seven feet, he's big enough to see over a defender harassing him on the sideline. Kawhi was set up on the perimeter, toward the other sideline, and Pascal, as the play called for, set a screen that allowed him to receive the ball.

If the Sixers had swarmed Kawhi, there may have been just enough time for him to find an open teammate to get a shot off before the buzzer. The pass and catch would have to be perfect.

But they played him straight up. With Ben Simmons guarding him, Kawhi dribbled to his right, then down the sideline and past our bench.

All our guys were standing up, both the players and assistant coaches. I was squatting and kind of down on my haunches as he came by. Simmons kept pushing Kawhi wider and wider and I wasn't sure Kawhi was going to be able to get a shot off before time ran out.

Just as he got to the right corner, just inside the three-point arc, Kawhi got a step on Simmons but Embiid came flying at him as he rose up for his shot. If you were a Sixers coach or fan, you could not have asked anything more of Embiid.

It was an incredible effort on his part. He shadowed Simmons and Kawhi all the way from the top of the arc and then got up off his feet to disrupt the shot without fouling.

Kawhi had to launch it really high, and as it was in the air, it looked like it was going to come up short—maybe even way short. It hit the front of the rim once—and then twice—and then hopped over to the other side—took another two bounces—and then fell through the net.

The bucket gave us a 92–90 victory. And it made history—it was the first time, in the whole seventy-year history of the NBA, that a Game 7 was decided by a buzzer beater.

It was an exciting, exhilarating, exhausting win. I was asked after the game what the win meant for the franchise, as if it were a crowning moment. And I understood that because what just happened was something you don't see very often.

But I replied that the most important thing was that we're still playing, and we still had room to grow. We were off to Milwaukee, where three days later we would begin a series with the Bucks, the team with the NBA's best record.

It's sometimes easier for me to sleep after a loss than a win because after a loss, I just want to close my eyes, shut it down, and start again the next day. After a win, I'm sometimes a little more revved up.

But I was pretty exhausted that night after Kawhi's buzzer beater. My wife, Roberta, had given birth about a week before to our second child, a boy we named Rocky. I went home, changed some diapers, and went to bed.

⌃

13

WE THE NORTH

THE RAPTORS ARE NBA CHAMPIONS

Being interviewed by Doris Burke while holding my son Leo after winning Game 6
against the Warriors. *(John W. McDonough / Sports Illustrated / Getty Images)*

I got strangely more relaxed the longer the playoffs went on. I'm sure part of it could have been that we didn't get knocked out early. I didn't actively think about that possibility, but as a coach, it has to be somewhere in the back of your mind because it's the worst of all possible outcomes.

But I also created this zone of calm around me. I didn't watch any TV news or ESPN highlight shows because I didn't want to hear any of the commentary on our games—not the pats on the back when we won or the critiques of why we lost. If I watched any of the other playoff series, it was with the sound turned down. I never look at social media and I obviously was not going to start then.

I spent quiet time at home with my wife and kids. I listened to music. (Our new house in Toronto has a room dedicated to that with an awesome sound system and a collection of 2,500 vinyl albums, including forty by Monk.) I went to the office earlier than usual, sometimes to be there alone watching tape, but also just to sit and play the piano.

It was a cool feeling because I knew the world around me was going crazy as we continued to advance, but as it all got noisier, I became calmer. During games, all I saw was the court, the players, and the couple of rows of fans in my view. I didn't look up or around.

There was one moment during the tense last seconds of a game at home when the rapper Drake, a Toronto native and a devoted Raptors fan, leaned over the scorer's table and gave me a quick back rub. If you watch it on video, it's hilarious. But I was completely unaware of it and had to be told later that it happened.

^

My sense of well-being certainly could have been tested by how the Milwaukee series began. In the first game, we quieted their home crowd by leading basically the whole first three quarters—and fairly comfortably. And then we got thumped in the last quarter. They outscored us 32–17 and won the game, 108–100.

That could have been deflating, but for me, it was encouraging. We proved to ourselves we could beat the Bucks on the road in an Eastern Conference Final. We just didn't finish the job.

I told the team: Okay, we just have to put a little more work in. Next game, how about if we play the whole forty-eight minutes?

But we didn't. We were down fourteen points at the end of the first quarter, twenty-five at the end of the half, and ended up losing, 125–103.

We were a step too slow all night on just about everything. We didn't contest shots. We gave them space, gave them confidence, and really let them settle in. We made a couple little runs but we had to play uphill the whole night.

We returned home in what most people would regard as a deep hole—down two games to none. But coaches don't think like fans or newspaper or TV pundits. We really can't. Our emotions don't swing (or they shouldn't). The cliché about not getting too high or too low really does apply. You have to move forward in some rational way.

When we regrouped in Toronto, I told the guys there was no

reason to panic. Through the season and into the playoffs, we had experienced some games like our Game 2 loss to the Bucks, where we just didn't play tough enough, our shots didn't fall, and it all snowballed. It happened and now we just needed to move on. I said I felt confident we were going to win the series, and I meant it.

Serge followed up with a long, great speech about being down two games to none to the Spurs in a Western Conference Final in 2016, when he was playing for Oklahoma City, and then roaring back to win four straight and take the series. It was a big moment for him in the film room.

I also made a couple of tactical changes.

Their star player, and the league's MVP, was Giannis Antetokounmpo, widely known as the Greek Freak, who at six foot eleven snares rebounds, dribbles full court, and barrels forward for layups and dunks with a power and grace that can seem unstoppable. A lot of people have this notion that you do one of two things against a player like him: guard him one-on-one and let him get his points but hold the other guys down, or send multiple defenders at him and make his teammates step up and beat you.

That was not my approach. I thought we could swarm him and make him give the ball up, and still scramble to defend their other threats. I told the team: We have to pack the paint better and not let him fly downhill at us and get all the way to the hoop. It will take multiple bodies to stop him. But when he passes, we're going to absolutely fly at their shooters and not let them bury us with three-pointers.

Pascal had been guarding Giannis. I made a change before Game 3 and put Kawhi on him as the primary defender. Pascal guarded Khris Middleton, their secondary scorer.

Because Giannis and Middleton did lots of two-way stuff—pick-and-rolls for each other, dribble handoffs—Pascal sometimes ended up back on Giannis anyway. But after he scored twenty-four and thirty points in the first two games, we held Giannis to just twelve in Game 3.

Our defensive effort did not exactly make the game easy for us. We did win, 118–112, but it took two overtimes to get the job done.

Kawhi Leonard scored eight points in the second overtime. On the night, he played fifty-two minutes (which was never envisioned in the load management plan), including the entire fourth quarter and every minute of both overtimes.

He basically lifted us on his shoulders and saved the season. A 2–0 deficit is manageable, but no NBA team has ever climbed out of a 3–0 hole. In addition to his defense, Kawhi scored thirty-six points. When I tried to get him a short break midway through the fourth quarter, he told me, "No, I'm good."

⌃

I've written about our player development. It never stops, not even deep into the postseason.

Freddy kept getting his shots blocked against Orlando. He was shooting from the corner—the so-called short corner and ordinarily the most desirable three-point shot to take. But defense tightens in the playoffs. He's just six feet tall, tiny by NBA standards, and much bigger guys were swatting his shots away as he released the ball.

After Freddy had three of his shots blocked in one game, I took him aside and said, "Dude, listen, we need your three-balls. So here's my idea. Get out of the corners. Stop shooting from there because they're getting too close to you. So how about this? Get out there on the arc, back up five more feet from the line, and let it fly from there."

He looked at me and said, "Okay."

That was it.

The next thing I know, before practices and after practices— before and after game-day shootarounds—he's out there shooting two hundred bombs at a time. He's just pumping away and they're going in.

We would go on to win Game 4 in Toronto against the Bucks, Game 5 back in Milwaukee, and then come home again and win Game 6. Four straight wins to close out the series. I told the team I was confident we would win the series and they went out and proved it.

It happened for lots of reasons. In Game 4, we got huge contributions from the bench, which allowed Kawhi to play a much more reasonable thirty-four minutes. Serge backed up his locker room pep talk with seventeen points and thirteen rebounds. Norman Powell had eighteen points. We were really crisp on offense, with thirty-two assists on forty-one buckets. (An assisted hoop is an indication of a team sharing the ball; an unassisted one is usually the result of a player going one-on-one.)

In Game 5, Kawhi lifted us with thirty-five points and in the clinching Game 6, he led us again with twenty-seven. We kept up and even tightened our suffocating defense on Giannis.

But probably the most astounding aspect of the last three victories was Freddy's shooting. My suggestion proved to be pretty good and his practice paid off.

In Game 4, he hit all three of his three-point attempts. In Game 5, he shot seven of nine. In Game 6, he shot four of five. That's fourteen for seventeen, or 82 percent—which is absurdly good shooting at any time in the season, let alone in three of the most pressure-filled games you can imagine.

^

Much of what we basketball coaches do is borrowed—or, depending on how you look at it, stolen. It's just how things work. You can't patent or copyright things in my business.

When I was looking for new out-of-bounds plays, a friend sent me some tapes of stuff that Rick Byrd, the longtime (and now retired) coach at Belmont University in Nashville, was running. I'm still using them. It's clever stuff. I don't know if Byrd was aware of it—or knew that there were like the equivalent of Belmont bootleg tapes circulating around.

I think much of what I did with the Rio Grande Valley Vipers was revolutionary, but it was built on what Chris Finch had started with the encouragement of the Rockets front office. I extended it, and what I began calling the shot spectrum is now accepted wisdom throughout the NBA.

You are twice as likely now to see a twenty-seven-foot jump shot at an NBA game than a sixteen-footer—the opposite of less than a decade ago when midrange shots were twice as common as long threes. Why? Because lots of other coaches and front offices saw that it worked. And they did the math and came to understand that it made sense.

I think the offense we run in Toronto is pretty cool, and some of it feels new. But when I coached the Canadian team at the FIBA World Cup in China over the summer, I saw numerous teams from around the world running elements of it.

If you asked me who the true visionaries have been in the years since I began my coaching career, I would name just a few: Tex

Winter and Phil Jackson for the triangle; Mike D'Antoni, the current Houston coach, for all his offensive innovations with the Rockets and before that, the Suns; and Dick Bennett, the long-time and now retired coach at the University of Wisconsin, for his defensive genius.

The other visionary I'd put on the list is Steve Kerr—the coach of our opponents, the Golden State Warriors, in the NBA Finals. After winning five titles as a player with the Bulls and Spurs, he moved into the front office of the Phoenix Suns, and then in 2014, became the coach of the Warriors.

He inherited a roster that included Steph Curry, Klay Thompson, and Draymond Green, but after he took over, they began passing the ball from angles no one had ever seen—and Curry shot it from previously unimaginable distances.

The Warriors were also a cultural phenomenon—Silicon Valley's team, a hoops start-up that seemed to have reimagined the geometry of basketball. When Kevin Durant, one of the league's top three players, signed with them as a free agent in 2016, it seemed almost unfair. The Warriors, in the minds of many people, were an unbeatable juggernaut. They had won three of the last four NBA titles. They were playing in their fifth consecutive NBA Finals.

I certainly didn't have Kerr's pedigree. In his NBA playing career, he had been teammates with Michael Jordan, Scottie Pippen, David Robinson, and Tim Duncan. (At Northern Iowa, I played alongside James Parker and Jason Reese. You've heard of them, right?)

No one on our Raptors roster could match the career achievements or celebrity status of the Warriors' big four of Curry, Durant, Green, and Thompson. Kawhi, who had won an NBA title with the Spurs, came the closest.

Durant was injured, but we expected him back before the

series was over. As Game 1 approached, I thought it was a good idea to directly address the high status and reputation of the team we were playing.

I did so with a couple of props that I pulled out during a film session. First, I put on a Los Angeles Rams hat. They happen to be my favorite football team, but they had just lost the 2019 Super Bowl to another legendary squad—the New England Patriots.

With my Rams hat on, I told our guys that I thought the NFC champs had gone into the Super Bowl too much in awe of the Patriots. All they seemed to talk about was how great the Pats were.

When all the hype ended and the game began, the Rams offense, which had been great all season long, was horrible. They eked out just a field goal in a 13–3 loss.

Then I put on a Philadelphia Eagles hat. I said the Eagles, in the 2018 Super Bowl, had respected New England but not so much that they didn't think they could beat them. They said all the right things and then went out and won the damn game.

Yeah, the presentation was a bit hokey, but I thought I needed to make the point, and a little bit of humor never hurts. (I got a big reaction from Kyle when I put on the Eagles hat. A Philly guy through and through, he grew up in the city and then played college ball there at Villanova.)

The Warriors' supposed invincibility was the elephant in the room. Before the series started, I wanted us to talk about it.

The series began with two games in Toronto. For the first, which took place on a Thursday night, our arena filled up early, with just about every one of the twenty thousand fans dressed in red.

Tens of thousands more gathered to watch on the big screens set up outside in what's known as Jurassic Park. Millions of television viewers were watching in the United States, of course—but also all across Canada.

The language and cultural divide between English and French speakers in Canada is normally mirrored in its sports preferences. You will not find many (if any) hockey fans who root for both the Toronto Maple Leafs and Montreal Canadiens. If one of those teams makes a good run in the NHL playoffs, there's a good chance that fans of the other team are rooting against them.

One of the great things about the 2018–19 season is that we became Canada's team. We kept picking up new fans as we rolled forward, and the excitement swept across all parts of the country and through the usual divides.

Our performance in Game 1 amped up the excitement to a new level. Any of our fans harboring doubts that we could really compete with the Warriors saw that we were up for the challenge and not intimidated.

Eight of our first nine shots were three-point attempts. I turned to someone on the bench after the first five minutes or so and said, "Have we taken a two yet?" Ordinarily, that might be too much long-range shooting, but I loved it.

I felt like the thing we had to do in the series is really go for it, and launching all of those threes—we made five in the first quarter—showed we had no hesitation. We were playing just like my old college coach, Eldon Miller, said we had to: without fear.

The confidence of our young guys was really something to behold. Fred came off the bench and played thirty-three minutes—starters' minutes—and scored fifteen points. He had the ball in his hands a lot and turned it over just once.

Where Fred was a calming influence through much of the game, Pascal was flat-out spectacular. Just two years after he and I came together in the gym after his rookie year ended—that day he said to me, "I've got to learn to shoot"—he lit the NBA Finals on fire.

Pascal scored thirty-two points, a new career high, on fourteen of seventeen shooting. He actually got off to a little bit of a slow start but hit nine of ten shots in the second half, including eight straight baskets at one point (spanning the entire third quarter and most of the fourth). He filled up the rest of the box score with eight rebounds, five assists, two blocked shots, and a steal.

If you were a casual NBA fan who was just tuning in for the Finals, you probably would have thought, *Who the hell is this guy?*

We had the lead almost the whole game—forty-three of the forty-eight minutes—and jumped out to lead in the series with a 118–109 victory.

An NBA team playing the first two games on the road in a seven-game series comes in with one goal: Steal at least one game on the other team's court. Turn the home court advantage in your favor.

After we beat the Warriors in the first game, the second one was really easy to analyze. We started out well enough, built a twelve-point lead midway through the second quarter, and went into halftime with a five-point lead. It was one of those games where Kawhi was carrying us. He kept drawing fouls and making his free throws. (He would end up sixteen for sixteen for the game.)

The Warriors have traditionally been really strong coming out of the locker room after halftime, and we weren't ready for it. They absolutely blitzed us. In the first five and a half minutes of the second half, they scored eighteen straight points, and our 59–54 lead became a 72–59 deficit.

This game was the series' first sighting of a box-in-one defense, which we put on Steph Curry.

Klay Thompson, Curry's fellow "Splash Brother" (they splash a lot of jump shots), landed badly after a shot attempt early in the fourth quarter and had to leave the game a couple of minutes later.

They were still without Durant, so we turned extra attention on Curry. We played him straight-up man-to-man, with Fred on him, and everyone else played zone. I did it again later in the series, and also played a little triangle and two—similar to the ZMT defense I pulled out two decades before in Birmingham, England.

You see those defenses every now and then in college or high school but never in the NBA. Well, you know what? It's still basketball. The players may be bigger and better, but the court is the same size, the passing angles don't change, the hoop is still round.

Curry laughed about the gimmick defense the first time he saw it from us and said he hadn't faced anything like it since seventh grade. "The whole fourth quarter, they were playing some janky defense," he said.

I laughed, too. It was janky, although I had not previously heard that word applied to an NBA tactic. (The phrase "junk defense" is more common.)

In that Game 2, after we fell way behind, Danny Green hit a three-pointer to close their lead to two points with twenty-six seconds left—and we just missed getting a steal on their next possession before Andre Iguodala hit a three-pointer to give the Warriors a 109–104 victory.

They had achieved what they came for, a victory on our home court—but our janky defense may have given them a little extra to think about.

⌃

The next two games would be at Oracle Arena in Oakland. I went into the locker room after the game fairly calm and told the team, "All right. We knew it was going to be a long series, right? Maybe six or seven games. All we've got to do now is get on the plane and do what they just did—take one from them on their home court."

As I've written a couple of times already, Kawhi has a habit of getting right to the heart of the matter. His game is direct. He moves from point A to point B with no wasted motion. The way he speaks is the same. No frills. No wasted words.

He stepped up when I was done and said, "Forget that." (He may have used a different f-word than "forget.") "We're not going out there to win one game. We're going to get them both."

He quickly moved back toward the corner of the locker room, with the rest of his teammates, and I said something like, "Yep, sounds good to me. What he said."

⌃

We had two days off before playing again. In one of our film sessions, I made them watch the whole eighteen-point run from the previous game. It wasn't pretty. The Warriors just kept coming down and scoring buckets.

Through the whole playoff run, we had some constants. Kawhi was certainly one. Kyle was always steady and really tough, and in numerous games, an explosive scorer. Whether he was shooting well or not, Fred almost always gave us a good floor game.

And then we had some players who stepped up and provided what we needed at just the right time. In Game 3, Serge Ibaka was the disruptive force we needed on defense. He blocked six shots and altered several more.

On offense, we played with a lot of freedom. I had a little talk with Kyle before the game, and he told me he was going to "let it rip." One of our players, I'm not sure who—Kyle said it was not him—wrote the same thing on the board before the game.

And that's exactly what we did. We were more fluid, with lots of cutting and passing that produced thirty assists on our forty-three buckets. We led just about wire-to-wire and came out with a 123–109 victory.

We were halfway to the challenge Kawhi laid down: take two games at Oracle.

There are lots of ways to analyze basketball games and figure out the factors that go into winning and losing. We look at all the metrics—how many total passes we make in a game; where on the floor our shots, and our opponents' shots, come from; what percentage of defensive possessions our players get their arms into the passing lanes; how often they deflect the ball.

But there are simpler things that are good indicators. For example, the game is played in four twelve-minute quarters, and if you can outscore the other team in most of those periods, you're probably going to win the series.

In the first three games of the series, we had won ten of the twelve quarters. In Game 4, we split the first two quarters and went into halftime down four points. Then we came out of the locker room and had a Warriors-like third quarter—one of those game-defining rallies they were known for. Kawhi scored seventeen points in the quarter, of his thirty-six for the game.

Serge was a monster. He's one of those players who builds on his own emotions, and when one element of his game falls into place, others follow. He followed his six blocked shots the previous game with twenty points.

Our 105–92 victory put us one game from being NBA champions.

Some of our fans may have expected that coming home to Toronto would be a coronation. Just get through the game and afterward, we'll have a trophy ceremony. I didn't see it that way and neither did our players.

One of the hardest things in sports is to get the fourth win to finish off a championship series. Momentum can be overrated. The other team—and especially a tough, proud champion like the Warriors—does not listen to the commentary saying that it looks like they're going down and decide to just roll over and die. Just the opposite. They dig in and make you earn it.

I started to tell the team about a series in Iowa when we came home needing to win just one game and, probably out of over-confidence, did not get the job done. We won it on the road.

I didn't get too far into the story before Kawhi cut me off. "You talking about the D-League?" he said. "I'm done hearing about the D-League."

The Warriors had fought us hard at the same time they were battling terrible injury problems. But Klay Thompson was back on the court at the start of Game 5, as was Kevin Durant, for the first time in the series.

The Warriors came out hot. Before five minutes had elapsed, they'd connected on five shots from beyond the arc—two each by Thompson and Durant, and one by Curry. As I would have expected, their stars were making a statement: *Not yet, Raptors.*

But in the second quarter, Durant went down with another injury—later diagnosed as a torn Achilles tendon. You could see it was bad when it happened. NBA players go at one another hard, but they are a fraternity.

Their players were shaken, and so were ours. After halftime, I saw Kyle go over to their bench to ask about Durant.

We were not really clicking and played from behind almost the whole game, but we never lost contact. By late in the fourth, we had pulled even, and with a little more than three minutes remaining, Kawhi hit a jump shot to give us a 103–97 lead.

At this point, we called a time-out. Our players seemed winded. It seemed like a moment to regroup and get an extra energy push.

What followed was a little coaching nightmare—my time in the harsh glow of the bright lights. Nothing good happened after the time-out. The Warriors went on a shooting spree, with Curry and Thompson bombing in balls from deep. They put together a 9–2 run and escaped with a 106–105 victory.

There are no counterfactuals in sports—no way to know what would have happened if we had not called that time-out. Maybe we would have powered forward and clinched it right there, on our home court. Or maybe the result would have been the same.

Some other people, though, seemed sure I had blown it. It's a good thing I wasn't watching TV. I now know that on one of those ESPN shows, they flashed a question on the screen, in big letters: DID NICK NURSE COST TORONTO GAME 5?

I'm sure plenty of other people were asking the same question.

⌃

Like in any big sporting event, there was all kinds of expert commentary preceding our matchup with the Warriors. The media members who cover the NBA closely tend to know the game and the league, so their batting average on getting things right isn't that bad.

But I'm pretty sure nobody predicted the visiting team was going to win four of the first five games. And now we were back in Oakland, hoping to win the series and the NBA championship on the road.

To top it off, there was lots of emotion around the venue, because win or lose, Game 6 of the series was going to be the Warriors' last in Oracle Arena, where they had played for nearly a half century. The franchise was moving into a new home across the bay in San Francisco.

You look to your veterans to step forward in games like this, especially at the start, when everyone might be a little on edge. Kyle Lowry was in his seventh season with the Raptors after beginning his career with Houston and Memphis. He was beloved in Toronto, the heartbeat of the franchise.

Less than two minutes into the game, the score was Lowry 8, Warriors 0. Kyle seemed to be sending a message that he had it handled. His first two points were on a strong drive to the hoop. The next six were on high-arching three-pointers. Both were pure as can be and hit nothing but net. (After the Warriors made a basket, Kyle hit another three-pointer, so he ended up scoring our first eleven points.)

Before long, though, we were in a dogfight. We led by one point at the end of the first quarter, three at the half, and then trailed by two at the end of the third quarter. Over the course of the game, the lead would change hands eighteen different times.

The composure of our young players was amazing. Freddy scored twelve of his twenty-two points in the game's last nine minutes. His final basket came on a three-pointer with just under four minutes remaining that put us ahead, 104–101. It was not from the corner, where he was getting his shots blocked, but from where I had told him to move to—straightaway and deep.

The Warriors kept coming at us, but we maintained the lead through the tense final minutes by making one big play after another. Serge scored after grabbing an offensive rebound. Kyle hit a fadeaway jumper from near the foul line that touched every part of the rim before falling through.

With twenty-eight seconds left, we were clinging to a 109–108 lead when Kyle fed the ball to Pascal about twenty feet from the hoop. The shot clock was running down and he was being guarded by Draymond Green, one of the toughest defenders in the NBA. If we didn't score, the Warriors would have the ball back needing just a two-point hoop to win.

I'm sure that Pascal's mind did not flash back to the end-of-game situation earlier in the season, against the Suns. There's no time for that. But everything builds. Having those opportunities, succeeding in them, prepares you for the next moment. A bigger moment.

Pascal took one dribble, followed by a big step to his left to get his shoulders past Green, and then feathered in what we call a floater—a shot off of one foot that is sort of half jump shot, half layup. I don't know how many people understand the touch required for that kind of shot—and the steely nerves it takes to sink it in the waning seconds of such a momentous game.

Steph Curry made a couple of foul shots to bring the Warriors within one—but then missed a three-pointer that would have put them ahead. Kawhi made three foul shots in the final seconds to give us a 114–110 victory.

We were the NBA champions.

The first one of the NBA's seventy-three champions, going back to the league's founding in 1946, to be based outside the United States.

And the first to be coached by a hoops vagabond from Carroll, Iowa, who fought his way up from a bunch of teams no one ever heard of in England—who came up through the D-League—and somehow reached the pinnacle of the basketball world.

EPILOGUE

If you could simulate my career trajectory in some kind of computer model, and run it, say, ten thousand times, how many would come up with my being an NBA coach? I'm not sure. Maybe none of them.

I was career-driven from the start—not some kid on a Eurorail pass hopscotching between countries and dabbling in basketball. I wanted to advance as a coach, to make it up to the NBA if at all possible. I just had an unusual way of going about it.

What I gained in my many stops was an absolute conviction that I could make teams better. I could win at basketball. It didn't matter the level I was coaching at or the names of the players, their salaries, or how many people were in the stands. At every step of the way I was learning. I was preparing for an opportunity that I knew might never come.

In the immediate aftermath of our title-clinching game at Golden State, I was asked by the media what winning an NBA championship meant to me—and what "my story," as one of the reporters put it, could mean to other people.

And honestly, it was hard to say amid the celebration and the bedlam. I had just come out of our locker room and my suit was soaked with champagne.

One thing I knew was that the plans we had put in place worked. The load management with Kawhi, and all the mental load management, too.

The players did not hear my voice any more than was necessary. I was the guy at the corner of the practice court, hat pulled down low, quietly observing and parceling out my words in small portions. Whenever I did speak, I think they listened.

We did not accept losses, either during the season or in the playoffs, but we never overreacted. We looked within ourselves, took stock, and tried to get a little better game by game, week by week.

Two months of playoff basketball is really long, but the players came in fresh and they never seemed tired, right to the end. They kept wanting the film sessions. They kept striving. They kept growing.

As for me, I've been able to look back some. I occasionally even did a little of that while it was all going on. After we won Game 3 against the Warriors in Toronto, I sat on the bench by myself for just a moment. My mom was on my mind. It would have been her ninety-fifth birthday, but she had passed away earlier in the season, while we were on a West Coast trip.

I thought about her and my dad, who died at eighty-nine in 2015. He got to see me make it into the NBA as an assistant, but not a head coach.

My dad retired early after I went off to Northern Iowa, so he and my mom could go to all my games, home and away. They put a lot of miles on the car. When the series was over, my thoughts went to a whole lot of other people who had helped me on the way up—coaches, teachers, teammates. Some of them, like Darrell Mudra, didn't really know how influential they were.

My celebration the night of the clinching game was really low-key. I spent it back at the hotel with a small group that included Nate, my nephew David, Steve Swanson—a coaching friend from England—and Frank Molak, one of my high school teammates. We all hung out. I played my keyboard a little bit.

It wasn't that much different than winning the state title game in Des Moines when I played for Kuemper Catholic. We ordered some pizzas and we laughed a lot.

It would be silly to say that winning the NBA championship was not the biggest moment in my professional life. Of course it was. In its scope—the global TV coverage, the twenty thousand people in the seats, the police motorcades to the arena, the privilege of coaching games that involve the best basketball talent on the planet—nothing can match it except another NBA title.

But for a sportsman, to use a British term, the satisfaction of winning any championship, anywhere—whether it's in Carroll, Iowa; Birmingham, England; or the Rio Grande Valley in Texas—does not outrank the satisfaction of winning any other championship. You achieved the ultimate, at whatever level you were competing. You threw your heart and mind into it.

You won the last game.

All I've wanted to be is a coach. To get better at the craft and to make individuals and teams better. I've found satisfaction and enjoyed the hell out of it anywhere that I've been afforded the opportunity to lead a team.

For anyone in any profession, the lesson has to be: Live in the present. Throw yourself into each day. And if anyone ever offers you a bigger job, you better make damn sure you've prepared yourself to succeed.

<hr />

June 2020

A short postscript seems appropriate here: In the months after I finished writing this book, and as it was being readied for publication, our world changed suddenly and dramatically. First came

COVID-19, which swept across the planet, took hundreds of thousands of lives, and shut down all semblance of normal life.

The pandemic was followed by a tragedy of a different kind: the death of George Floyd, an African-American man in Minneapolis, Minnesota, at the hands of a white police officer who kept him pinned to the pavement, with his knee on his neck, for nearly nine minutes. This horrific act, recorded on cellphone video, repulsed all people of good faith and caused protests and civil unrest on a scale America has not seen since the 1960s.

I am under no illusions. I'm a basketball coach. But I do hope, humbly, that I can in some small way contribute to bringing people together. One of the big themes of this book has been lifelong learning. Here is a situation where we are all learning as we try to make our way forward. We are trying to listen to and care for one another.

Our roster on the Toronto Raptors is composed of players from a half dozen nations and three continents. We play in a big, diverse international city. Our players contribute in significant ways to the fabric of Toronto as well as to their home cities and nations, and I try to do the same. (The Nick Nurse Foundation supports children and young adults through music, sports, and literacy programs.)

Across the NBA, our players and many of our coaches have strong opinions, and they speak out forcefully for social justice. I'm proud of that. Our league engages with the world, and even on the court, we are a living example of people from vastly different backgrounds who come together for a common cause.

We sure do need a lot of that right now. I'll do my part. In the meantime, I am praying for everyone's good health. And for peace and justice.

ACKNOWLEDGMENTS

This book would not have become a reality without Brandon Hurley, David Black, and Michael Sokolove. Brandon came to me and brought me to David, and David brought us to Michael. It was a true joy working with them on this endeavor. Thank you, as well, to Philip Marino and everyone at Little, Brown.

Thanks to my brothers and sisters: Jim, Dan, Sue, Tom, Ken, Shelley, Steve. It was an amazing, dynamic experience to grow up with you all, and it totally shaped my path.

I would also like to thank all the cousins on both sides of my parents' families: the Nurses and the Shoemakers. A shout-out to Bob Wiess, who was and is a big supporter and friend.

Special thanks to Geni Melville, Adrian Griffin, Nate Bjorkgren, and Sergio Scariolo: my right-hand men and women. Jim Sann, Jon Goodwillie, Patrick Mutombo, Tyler Marsh, Phil Handy, Jeremy Castleberry, John Corbacio, Jamaal Magloire, John Bennett, and Jama Mahlalela have been invaluable assistant coaches—along with Trevor Pridie, Fabulous Flournoy, Mark Tyndale, and Brittni Donaldson.

I would like to thank Larry Tanenbaum and the Maple Leaf Sports and Entertainment board of directors, Wayne Embry, Masai Ujiri, Bobby Webster, Teresa Resch, and Dan Tolzman, for giving me such a wonderful opportunity with the Raptors, and for their unparalleled leadership. And to the many others who work within the Raptors organization, all of whom give a championship effort day in and day out. Thank you from the bottom of my heart.

I must thank *all* the players I have coached on all the teams all over the world, meaning the stars, the starters, and the bench guys on the rosters of:

      Derby Rams
      Grand View University
      University of South Dakota
      Birmingham Bullets
      Telindus Oostende, Belgium
      Manchester Giants
      London Towers
      Oklahoma Storm
      Brighton Bears
      Iowa Energy
      Rio Grande Valley Vipers
      Toronto Raptors
      Great Britain National Team
      Canadian National Team

All these players sacrificed and cared, and we learned and worked together. The magnitude of your efforts will remain with me for life.

There are so many other people along the way who have been instrumental in my success, more than I can possibly list here.

Lastly, I am grateful to my teammates at the University of Northern Iowa and Kuemper Catholic High School. We played D, moved the ball, and cared about winning.

INDEX

Note: Italic page numbers indicate photographs.

basketball (in general) (*cont.*)
D-League teams, 75–77, 80–86
film sessions, 125–126
geometry in, 126
getting fourth win in championship series, 233
human interactions in, 31–32
intensity of effort in, 82–83, 86–87
point guards, 22–23, 103–105
"positionless," 50
shooting, 33–36, 78–79
shot spectrum, 110–114, 121, 158, 225
teaching how to play, 81
three-point shots, 108–109, 111–114
trades, 81–82
triangle offense, 48–50
true visionaries in, 225–226
in United Kingdom, 43
basketball laboratory, Rio Grande Valley Vipers as, 110–112, 116–117
BBL. *See* British Basketball League
Beckham, David, 167
Belgian Cup, 59
Belichick, Bill, 157
Belmont University, 225
Bennett, Dick, 226
Bennett, Tony, *25*
Berry, Jim, 31, 32–33
Bezos, Jeff, 157
Bird, Larry, 109
Birmingham, England, 45
Birmingham Bullets, *145*
coaching psychology with, 93–94
experimentation with, 50–53
liquidation of, 65
mindset of, 45–47
Bjorkgren, Nate
with Iowa Energy, 84–85
at playoffs celebration, 241
with Raptors, 176
with Santa Cruz, 118
as young coach, 86

Blind Pig offense, 69
Boots, Dave, 41, 126
Bosh, Chris, 132
Boston Celtics, 132, 169
Boucher, Chris, 40, 178
box-in-one defense, 230
Brighton, England, 66
Brighton Bears, 66–72
author's ownership of, 7–8
demise of, 71–72
Rodman's games with, 67–71
work done in schools by, 66–67
Brissett, Oshae, 40, 178
British Basketball League (BBL)
author's coaching in, 63–64
history and financial twists of, 64–65
London Towers' championship in, 66
and Rodman with Brighton Bears, 70–71
Brooklyn Nets, 130, 132–134
Brown, Brett, 210
Brown, Freddie "Downtown," 109
Brown, Hubie, 214
Brown, Larry, 21, 23
Brown, PJ, 132
Bryant, Kobe
and Jackson, 151
midrange shots by, 111, 113
Bucknall, Steve, 51
Budweiser Basketball League, 65
Burke, Doris, *219*
Butler, Jimmy, 209–211, 213–215
Byrd, Rick, 225

Canadian national team, 61, 225
Canadian sports preferences, 228
Carlsberg Basketball League, 65
Carroll, DeMarre, 137
Carroll, Iowa, 11–13
Carroll, Pete, 157, 175
Casey, Dwane
author on staff of, 122–123

ABOUT THE AUTHORS

Nick Nurse is an American basketball coach and is currently coaching the Toronto Raptors in the NBA. He was born on July 24, 1967, in Carroll, Iowa.

Michael Sokolove is a longtime contributing writer for the *New York Times Magazine* and the author of seven previous books.